SUGARBALL

A Novel of Negro League Baseball

R. Lee Procter

Black Rose Writing | Texas

The author grants the final approval for this literary material.

First printing

This is a work of fiction. Names, characters, businesses, places, events, and incidents are either the products of the author's imagination or used in a fictitious manner. Any resemblance to actual persons, living or dead, or actual events is purely coincidental.

ISBN: 978-1-68513-003-9
PUBLISHED BY BLACK ROSE WRITING
www.blackrosewriting.com

Printed in the United States of America
Suggested Retail Price (SRP) $22.95

Sugarball is printed in Sabon

*As a planet-friendly publisher, Black Rose Writing does its best to eliminate unnecessary waste to reduce paper usage and energy costs, while never compromising the reading experience. As a result, the final word count vs. page count may not meet common expectations.

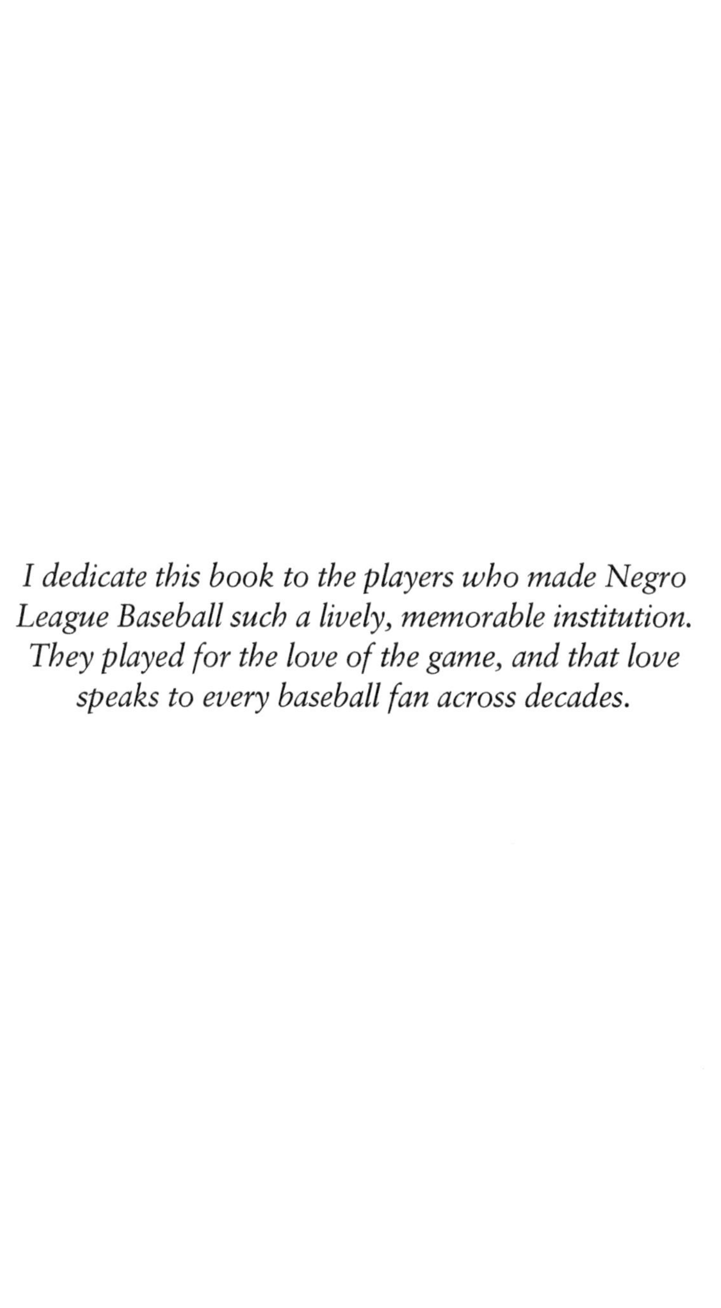

I dedicate this book to the players who made Negro League Baseball such a lively, memorable institution. They played for the love of the game, and that love speaks to every baseball fan across decades.

SUGARBALL

CHAPTER ONE

September 24, 1937

My name is Clyde Wiggins, but everybody calls me "Peanut" 'cuz I've always been small for my age, 'cept now I'm a tick under 5 feet tall, which is just about average for a twelve year old and big enough to play crackerjack shortstop on the sandlots, when I have the time. I love baseball. I love baseball more than I love Christmas day, hot chocolate and the last day of school combined. I love baseball more than I love my mother, and I love her a lot. I love baseball the way my boss, Mr. Gus Greenlee, loves money. Mr. Greenlee is the greatest man I know, and a personal friend of mine. He owns the Pittsburgh Crawfords, the greatest team in all of baseball, not just the Negro National Leagues. I am the biggest fan of the Crawfords in all Western Pennsylvania, which is how I almost came to be stabbed. Here's how that happened.

I run numbers for Mr. Greenlee, who is the owner of the biggest, richest numbers bank in Pittsburgh, which is how he got to be so important. What I do is "run the circuit" – collect numbers and bets from customers. I run from the Hurricane Lounge over to the Savoy Ballroom, then down to the Bamboola Club, across the street to Goode's Pharmacy, next door to the LaSalle Beauty Salon, and then on to the Harlem Casino, the Pythian Temple, the Center Avenue Elks and finally to Duke Perry's Pool Hall. Every sportin' man and woman on the Hill – that's where I work and live, "The Hill," also known as Little Harlem – has his or her personal three numbers, like, say 4-8-5. When I come by, my customers give me their numbers, and a bet – usually a nickel or dime, but sometimes as much as a dollar. I put the money in the special pockets my mom has sewn inside my pants, and I file the numbers in my head, so if the police get me, there's no evidence. The winning numbers are in the next day's paper – the last three numbers of the New York Stock Exchange total. The winning numbers pay off 600 to 1. Bet a dime, win 60 bucks. Sweet.

A lot of my customers also use bookies to bet on Crawfords games. I'm very popular with these folks, because I am the Editor-In-Chief, Senior Reporter, Head Writer, and Sole Distributor of the "Crawford Courier," a weekly one-sheet handout of hot inside news about the Crawfords. The white newspapers hardly ever cover our games, and they never run box scores and keep statistics, which is why my paper is a must-read. Today's headline is, "Gibson Clubs Twin

Roundtrippers In 9-1 Crawfords Romp – Paige Sparkles."

> DATELINE GREENLEE FIELD – Gus Greenlee's first place horsehiders routed their crosstown rivals the Homestead Grays this past Wednesday 9-1 in an afternoon romp before 3,769 Iron City diamond bugs.
>
> Crawford powerhouse Josh Gibson raised his average to .361 with three hits, including mammoth clouts in the 5th and 7th innings that raised his Negro National League-leading home run total to 23.
>
> Mound honors went to fireballing ace twirler Leroy "Satchel" Paige, who notched his 13th victory against 4 losses, and lowered his circuit-best earned run average to 1.77.

After I run the circuit, I look every which-way as I head back to the Crawford Grill, Mr. Greenlee's headquarters. I give every name and hand every penny to the policy banker, Mister Benny Melrose, a very skinny and sad looking man who wears a translucent emerald green eye-shade and sleeve garters and chews on cheap cigars that he hardly ever lights.

If I don't hand in the money by 2 p.m., Mr. Melrose sends somebody out to look for me. This fella's name is Gorilla Smith, a friend of Mr. Greenlee's. Gorilla's an ex-prize fighter who had to retire after his he got his bell rung by Ace Lennox in a championship bout. He once told me that if I even THOUGHT about pilfering a day's take, he'd pound me into the ground like a circus tent peg. I understand this. It's nothing personal with Gorilla. He needs the job, and he'd pulverize any of Mr. Greenlee's runners who tried to dash with his cash. Gorilla is also a friend of Mr. Greenlee's. He gives me Juicy Fruit when he has a fresh pack.

The key to being a successful numbers runner is to move fast and keep your mind on what you're doin', which I usually always do. The only exception was this one particular day, because someone had pasted a giant poster on the sidewall of the Coobus Club, right next to Perry's Pool Hall on Sycamore Street. There it was, in giant black letters on a yellow and orange background:

One Day Only! One Game Only!
2:30 p.m., Friday, September 24 – Beautiful Greenlee Field
The Greatest Baseball Exhibition Ever Staged On Any Field Anywhere!

Dizzy Dean's Major League All-Stars Versus Satchel Paige and the Pittsburgh Crawfords!
Dean Versus Paige in a Mighty Pitchers' Duel!
Josh Gibson Versus Mickey Parnell in an Awesome Slugfest!
Adults – 50 cents, Children 10 and Under – 10 cents.
ONE GAME ONLY to Decide Who is the Best In Baseball!

There's Satch at the top of his wind-up, kicking his foot above his head so high it blocks out the sun. There's Dean flinging a fireball. There's muscular Mickey Parnell belting a home run for the St. Louis Browns. And there's Josh Gibson, connecting for an epic fence-buster. I'm staring at Josh's picture, thinking about where I can scare up 50 cents (or can I pretend I'm under 10 and get in for a dime) when I hear a voice that makes my blood freeze and my heart drop into my shoes. "Well, if it ain't my ol' pal Peanut."

When I turn around, I see a very nasty looking "Arkansas toothpick" pointed directly at my throat. Only one young man of my acquaintance carries a foot-and-a-half long knife, and can kill a man by throwing it or stabbing with it. That would be Chester Polk – a six foot, one inch bad attitude behemoth who, last time I heard, was locked up in the Eastern Pennsylvania Reform School for Negro Law-Breakers. I can see Chester's gold front tooth as he grins at me – always a bad sign. Behind Chester are his two half-as-tall-but-twice-as-wide playmates, Slick and Bumpy. "Now I believe," growls Chester, "that it's getting along about 2 o'clock. Which means Peanut here done collected every dime he's gonna collect for Mister Gus Greenlee. We'll have that money, Peanut, elst I'm gonna cut you three ways – long, deep and wide."

"I don't know what you talkin' 'bout." I know that's weak, but it's the best I can do with a frozen brain. When a knife is 2 inches from your nose, it looks like a broadsword.

"You know how to dance, Peanut?"

"Dance?"

"Yeah. Tap dance. Like Mr. Bojangles Robinson. Let's have us some fancy tap dancing," says Chester. Uh oh. Any dancin' I do, they'll hear the ching-ching-ching of nickels and dimes in my pockets. I open my mouth to object, but that knife backs me up against the wall. Next thing I know I'm bobbin' up and down, sounding like the sleigh bells on Santa's reindeer. "My, my my," says Chester. "How much you think he's got, Slick?"

"Fifty dollars at least."

"Bumpy?"

"Maybe sixty."

"If I give you what I got," I squeak, "Mister Greenlee's gonna have Gorilla Smith use me for a punchin' bag." Chester pulls back slightly, in mock horror.

"I never said nothin' about you givin' us that money, my man. We gonna take it ourselves." He lowers the knife to my waist. "By cuttin' off those raggedy pants of yours."

Somehow, this strikes me as even more horrifying than being knifed. "I can't be runnin' around the Hill without no britches on! My mama would kill me." Chester busts out laughing at this, and his two goons follow suit.

"You gonna fight us, Peanut?" said Chester. "Because we want to go to this here ballgame just like you. And if you fight us, I'll have to do to you what I did to Dempsey McGee." Dempsey McGee was a runner just like me, only older, bigger and tougher. Chester stuck that knife in his chest to get his day's take. That's what got him sent to reform school.

"I…I don't want that."

"Too late, Peanut. All in all, I think it'd be a whole lot easier getting those pants if you weren't breathin'…." And with that Chester moves in with that knife, aimed straight at my heart.

"*What's all this mess? What's goin' on here?*" The most beautiful voice I ever heard echoes through that alley. Chester, Slick and Bumpy turn around. The giant silhouette turns into a man-mountain of scowling rock-hard muscle as it comes toward us. When I see who it is, my heart nearly explodes. It's the greatest baseball player in the world. The black Babe Ruth. The Dusky King of Clout. The Bronze Behemoth. There stands Mister Josh Gibson, star slugger of the Pittsburgh Crawfords, lugging a khaki canvas bag filled with his 50-ounce bats. He grabs one and lets the others clatter to the cobblestones. Chester turns the knife on Josh as the two lock eyes. Slick and Bumpy both flick open switchblades as they get a fix on Josh. All I can do is stare and pray.

CHAPTER TWO

"Nothin' for you here, Josh," says Chester. "This ain't your fight. Just a little monetary transaction between Mr. Peanut Wiggins and myself."

"Uh huh." Josh never once looks at that knife – just keeps staring into Chester's eyes. "Know what the secret of home run hitting is, young man? Don't usually give away my secrets, but I think you oughta know."

"What?" says Chester. The swagger is gone, replaced by a twitchy distress.

"Quickness. Not speed. Different from speed. Satchel Paige throws me that nasty fastball…" And with that, Josh smashes Chester's hand, sending that knife a hundred feet down the alley. "…I gotta be quick. It's my business."

"Ahhhhhh! Dang!" Chester's hand is busted pretty bad, and his pride is busted up even worse. "Get him! And get the money!" he orders his soldiers. Josh has the bat back on his shoulder. He turns toward Slick and Bumpy. They look at him, look at

Chester's hand, and then fold up their switchblades as they back out of the alley. Josh watches them go. Chester stares at Josh, then scuttles backwards after his pals, his purpling right hand dangling, useless, from his wrist. Josh slides his bat back in his bag, and starts to walk away.

"Hey!" I shout. "Wait for me!"

So now Josh is stride walking down Central Avenue toward the Crawford Grill, and I'm running to keep up with him. Everybody we pass gives him a friendly shout-out.

"How many homers ya gonna hit today, Josh?"

"Hey, Josh! You and Satchel show them white boys what we can do!"

"Show that Dizzy Dean what a real slugger looks like!"

I add my two cents. "We're gonna take 'em today, aren't we Josh?" He stops so quickly that I crash into his legs and just barely stay upright.

"What you doin', messin' with them boys? They like to kill you, Peanut." He's angry. I'm surprised he knows my name. Did he hear it from Chester?

"I'm real careful, usually. I...I...guess I got sidetracked. Had my mind on the big game today." Josh bends over till his face is in mine.

"You got to stay in your own business, son." He pokes me in the chest to emphasize the word "business." "I'm gonna walk you to the Grill so some other gangster don't carve you up like a Christmas ham before you can drop off that cash. My salary's in there someplace."

The Crawford Grill looms over Wylie Street like a giant gilded castle the size of an airship hangar. Imagine the Loew's Penn movie palace, but instead of just showing movies this place has a restaurant and bar on the first floor, a dance hall on the second and a private club on the third. The dance hall has Pittsburgh's only revolving stage so that the Earl Hines band can start up even before the Count Basie band stops playing. The private club is Mr. Gus Greenlee's very own Club Crawford, where the *real* business gets done. I never been on the third floor, but my mama works there, serving drinks. She told me that Louis Armstrong likes Iron City Beer. I tasted a beer one time. I thought it was putrid. My mama told me it was an acquired taste. If something tastes as bad as that, why would you want to acquire it?

Speaking of Mama, she sees me with Josh as we walk through the kitchen on our way to the numbers bank. She's loading four smothered pork chop blue-plate specials on her platter as we pass. Her smile fades to a grimace as she looks at Josh. I try not to look guilty, but it doesn't work. She knows I got myself into some kind of dicey shenanigans.

I'm dumping handfuls of dimes and nickels into Benny's coin sorter when Mister Gorilla Smith comes in with another of Mr. Gus Greenlee's associates, Mister "Bonecrusher" Doaks, also an ex-prizefighter who is even bigger and meaner-looking than Gorilla. Bonecrusher puts his meathook on my right shoulder and says in his deepest basso profundo, "Mister Gus Greenlee requests the pleasure of your company in his office." Gulp. He's looking at me like he's the ax, I'm the turkey, and Thanksgiving is tomorrow.

"Whatever you say, Mister Doaks."

Josh and I are escorted via Mister Gus Greenlee's personal elevator into his executive office on the third floor, and my stomach drops into my shoes. Only three times in my life have I felt like I was in a place built by angels 'cuz God might come down and pay a visit. The first time was the Gimbel Brothers Department Store, where my mama took me to meet Santa Claus when I was six. Second was Mister Andrew Carnegie's Public Library, where my mama took me to get my library card when I was nine. The third is this place here. I feel like I'm meeting the President of the United States.

Mister Gus Greenlee is signing some papers on a desk so big you could land an airplane on it. Behind him is a painting of himself that's three times as big as he is in real life. Gorilla and Bonecrusher slip out and close the door behind them. Without looking up, Mister Gus Greenlee says, "Have a seat." Josh and I walk the half city block to the green velvet overstuffed armchairs in front of the desk. Josh stands, but I sit. Mistake. I sink so far into the cushions I can barely see over the top of the desk. Gus finally looks up at us, settling on Josh. "Heard you boys got into a fracas."

"Couple of hooligans jumped Peanut here."

Gus looks at me. "That so?" I nod, too scared to say anything.

"Chester Polk and his boys. In an alley," says Josh. "Peanut was trying to fight 'em off, but there was three of 'em. With knives. I walked by, saw he needed a hand."

Gus gets up and walks around his desk. "You done good, Josh. I appreciate it." Gus puts his arm around him and walks him toward the door. He takes a folded-up bill out of his vest pocket, unfurls it and hands it to Josh. "For services rendered."

Josh looks at the bill. Then he re-folds it and tries to put it back into Greenlee's vest. "Just helpin' out my friend Peanut. No big deal." But Gus stops him. "Gus Greenlee pays his debts. The grapevine is abuzz. Word on the street says you don't fuss with Gus, that his boys are on the case. That's the way it's got to be." Josh takes the bill, looks at Gus, then walks back over to me. "Give this to your mama." As he leaves, I look at the bill. One hundred dollars. It'd take me four months to make that sum. I have never seen such a big number on a single piece of paper in my life. My heart is thumping in my chest, and that's before I realize that Mister Gus Greenlee and I are all alone in his office. He's standing over me, arms crossed.

"What really happened?"

"Well, I..."

"Were you takin' care of business, Peanut?"

"Well..."

"We talked 'bout this. 'Bout you keepin' your mind on business."

"I know, Mr. Greenlee, but..."

"You were daydreamin', weren't you, young man?"

"I...I was just lookin' at this poster for today's game..." Mister Gus Greenlee lets out a loud, disgusted sigh, walks back around and sits at his desk. He lets me stew in my own juice as he lights one of his big cigars. "Don't think you're cut out for this line of work, Peanut."

NO! I need this job! I leap to my feet and lean over his desk. "Mister Greenlee, I goofed up this one time, but I'll never, ever mess up again as long as I live. Ever ever ever. You can count on me one hundred percent."

"Can I, Peanut? What if Josh hadn't been there today?"

"But he WAS!"

"But he won't always, will he?" Mister Gus Greenlee has me there. He looks me right in the eye. "My organization – we're like a family, Peanut. A big happy family. Well, sometimes not so happy, but you know what I mean. And I'm the daddy."

"Uh huh." He IS like my daddy. Has been ever since my own daddy passed away in the Great Pittsburgh Flood two years ago. He's given me a chance, pays me a decent wage, looks after me.

"I take care of my family, Peanut. I see one of my boys – a good boy, most of the time, but a little bit dreamy – he puts his life in danger 'cuz he can't take his mind off baseball, I start in to worry."

"'Bout what, Mister Greenlee?"

"That he might get himself bumped off. And then I wonder."

"Wonder?"

"'Bout how such a person could be helpful to me in another capacity."

"Like what?"

Greenlee half-smiles and lowers his voice to a husky whisper. "Well, Peanut, I could use a person – someone smart – on the Crawfords. Someone on the *inside*, who the players might tend to overlook. Someone with his eyes and ears *open*. Know what I mean? Someone who could tell me things about…things."

"What kind of things?"

Mister Gus Greenlee walks around his desk, leans over and smiles at me. "Oh, I don't know. Things. Like, for example, what kind of mood Brother Satchel Paige is in. If he's happy with the Crawfords, or if he…well, Brother Satchel is easily led. By unscrupulous swindlers who want to bribe him to jump the team and barnstorm for them. I'd like to know about that."

"You…you want me to…to be a spy?" Mister Gus Greenlee laughs. "Not as such, Peanut. It's just that if you were to become the batboy for the Crawfords…"

My heart almost leaps out of my chest. "Batboy? With a uniform and everything?"

Gus nods. "Jimmy Hubbard's daddy is a Pullman porter, got him on as a shoeshine boy at the station. Jimmy quit, and the position of Crawfords batboy is vacant. How'd you like the job?"

CHAPTER THREE

"How'd you like the job?"

You mean the chance to hang around my favorite place in the whole entire world? Get right up close to the game, so I could really see how it's played? Hang out with Satchel Paige, and get so close I can hear the sizzle on his "bee ball?" Feel the dirt fly off the spikes of Cool Papa Bell as he races from first to third on a bunt single, and then steals home? Have my eardrums busted by the crack of Josh Gibson's bat as he drives a ball higher and farther than anyone ever hit a ball before, and that includes the great Babe Ruth? Get to see every single Crawfords game, and actually get paid for it???

"Ummm...yeah. I think that'd be all right," I say. Mister Gus Greenlee lets out a loud, long guffaw. He can see right through me.

"As long as your mama says it's okay." Mama! I swallow hard.

"Would...uhh...would you be willing to ask her?" Mister Gus Greenlee ponders this.

"You need to be the one," he says. "But ain't no reason I can't ask a couple of the boys to help, I guess. Josh, for sure. And Cool Papa."

"Cool Papa Bell?" Cool Papa Bell is the best center fielder in baseball history, and also the Manager.

"Cool Papa can be pretty persuasive...when he wants to be. If you want the job..."

"I want the job, you bet!" I say, a little louder than I want.

"Then you start today. Call it a tryout. Try to make a good impression at the game."

"Yes sir! You bet I will! Thank you, Sir. THANK YOU!" I reach out to shake his hand, and he pulls me into big bear hug, just like my daddy used to give me.

He lets me go and says, "Eyes and ears OPEN, Peanut! Hear me?" I nod and race out the door. I run flat out till I turn up Bedford Avenue, and then I stop and stare. Wow. My spine starts to crackle with that great shivery ballpark feelin'. There it is – beautiful Greenlee Field, pride of the Negro Leagues and smart showcase of the Negro League Champion Pittsburgh Crawfords. My daddy and I had bleacher seats on the day this ballpark opened. My daddy looked at that glorious emerald field and said, "Son, if a black man can build himself a ballpark like this in the middle of the Depression, ain't nothin' that black folk like us can't do. Nothin'. Remember that." I think of my daddy as I by-pass the turnstiles and walk right up to the "Players Entrance." Sleepy-eyed Frog Rawlins is on the door, and he's ready to turn me away for the umpteenth time when I hear myself speak the words I've waited my whole life to say. "Lemme in, Frog. I'm with the team."

"You?!?" He thinks I'm ribbing him.

"That's right."

"Sez who?"

"Sez Mister Gus Greenlee. Jimmy Hubbard quit. Looks like I'm the new batboy of the champion Pittsburgh Crawfords." Frog stares at me, wondering if I'd really have to nerve to make this up. Then he steps aside and I open the door to heaven.

You'd think I'd have a million golden memories of my very first game as batboy for the Crawfords. Truth is, all I could think about was trying to prove to Cool Papa Bell and the Crawfords players that I was just what they wanted as a permanent batboy. I do remember the tingle up my spine as I trotted out on that emerald diamond for the first time. *The mown-hay smell of the fresh-cut grass baking in the sunlight, crunching under my feet...the women in their Sunday church dresses and the men in their white shirts, neckties, and straw boaters...the players, like gods, throwing it faster and hitting it farther than humanly possible...and the sounds! When you're on the field, you can hear it all – the players heckling each other, the fans buzzing when a big slugger steps in, and the umpire bellowing "Steeee-rike Threeeee!"*

I did every single thing the players wanted, and then some. I hustled bats back to the dugout. I ran balls out to the umpire. I handed out towels to players as they came into the dugout, and took their chewing tobacco pouches when they went back out. When Josh told me that Satchel Paige might like an icy lemonade after the 5th inning, I got him one before he could ask, and he tipped me a dollar.

I almost got killed in the 9th inning. We had two outs, score tied, Cool Papa Bell on 3rd base. Dizzy Dean reared back and fired a bullet. Little Willie Tatum, the rookie, swung over the ball, and hit a colossal "Baltimore chop" that kangarooed thirty feet in front of home plate. Then he dropped his bat right in the third base path and took off for first. 'Course Cool Papa took off as soon as ball hit bat, and he's the man who – as Josh once said – "*could get out of bed, turn the lights out across the room, and be back under the covers before it got dark.*" Long story short, it all happened at once – me lunging for the bat, Cool Papa diving headfirst for home, and the catcher clutching the ball and whipping around to tag him. Only the catcher tagged *me*, 'cuz I accidentally got in between him and Cool Papa. Cool Papa bounced off me and fell flat on home plate with the winning run. The mighty Crawfords won 2-1, the catcher went wild and screamed his head off at the umpire, Dizzy Dean smiled and shook his head, and I got carried off the field on the shoulders of Cool

Papa Bell and Deacon Powell, who was in the on-deck circle.

Turns out that was the easy part. Now I have to talk to mama about switching jobs and becoming a full-time batboy.

CHAPTER FOUR

I'm standing right at the back door of the Crawford Grille kitchen waiting for Mama's shift to end. I can hear music from the second floor – the Jimmie Lunceford band playing, "I'm Walking Through Heaven With You." When Mama was still a dancer she had a featured solo during this number. She finally bustles out the door and I force a smile. "Hey, Mama!"

"Peanut! What are you doing here? Are you okay? Is something wrong? Why did Mr. Greenlee want to talk to you?'

"I-I had a little dust-up with some guys but it all turned out okay and look what I got for you!" I pull out the hundred-dollar bill and put it in her hand. I thought she'd be happy, but she's shocked. "Where did you get this, Peanut? Tell me! NOW!"

Josh steps forward. "I gave it to him, Lila. Couple of hooligans jumped him for his numbers money. I stepped in. Gus thanked me with that bill. I hardly did a thing, so I gave it to Peanut to give to you."

Mama looks up at Josh. She looks like she's gonna cry. "Thank you, Josh." Then she turns to me. "Peanut, this job is too dangerous. You're going to quit."

"I already DID quit, Mama! Or rather, Mister Gus Greenlee fired me. But then he made me the full-time permanent batboy for the Crawfords!"

"Did he now? Without my permission?"

Cool Papa steps forward. "That's why we're here, Delilah. I'm Jimmy Bell. Fellas call me 'Cool Papa.' I play centerfield, help coach the team. We'd really like it if Peanut here…" Even before he can finish, Mama cuts in.

"There is no way on God's green earth I'm going to let my boy join that bunch of rascals and learn their wicked ways. How will Peanut go to school? Who will look after him? I know these players. They come into the Grille to drink and gamble and chase the chorus girls..."

I can't help it. I pipe up, "I don't go to school *now*, Mama!" Whoops. Wrong thing to say. She knows this, and I know she knows it because she knows where the money I give her comes from, but doin' and sayin' are two different things. Luckily, Cool Papa speaks up. He has a friendly voice and a calm way, just like Mama's own daddy before he passed.

"I always carry some books with me, Mrs. Wiggins. The Bible. Charles Dickens. Shakespeare. If you let him join us, I'll see that he reads every day. And as for his numbers, I'll let Peanut keep the scorebook and figure out the team averages to give to the sportswriters. No game has more mathematics than baseball."

"What about those reprobate players?" Mama is still angry, but I can feel her softening just a little. Maybe there's hope.

"Mrs. Wiggins, let me speak honestly," says Cool Papa. He takes a deep breath, lets it out, and looks her dead in the eye. "Your son was running numbers for Gus Greenlee. If he doesn't join our team, he'll probably run numbers for somebody else. Every single day he'll come in contact with gamblers, pool players, and petty criminals. Peanut himself is...well, he's not a criminal, no way, but...how can I say this...he's learning to move in the shadows. Do you understand?"

"Yes, but..." Cool Papa moves closer to her, and takes her hand. He softens his tone of voice even more.

"What's next for him, Lila? If he's lucky, he might take over a policy book, or collect debts for a loan shark. This batboy job takes Peanut out of that world. He'll be in the fresh air, doing good, honest work, helping a bunch of fellas play baseball. He'll get room and board on the road, and we'll pay him ten dollars a week that he'll send home to you. And that's one less mouth you'll have to feed."

"Well...." Oh my goodness...is she going to say yes? I think so, but then her face clouds over and she starts to shake her head. Josh speaks up.

"I'll look after him, Lila." My mom looks up at him.

"Promise?"

"Proved that today. Ain't nothin' gonna happen to him when I'm around. And I'll make sure I'm around. Got my word on that."

"I believe you, Josh. But he's my only boy. When I look at him, I see my late husband Frank. I just don't know if I could live without Peanut around the house."

"Mama, please..." I say, but before I say more Josh puts his hand on my shoulder.

"Think about it, Delilah," says Cool Papa. "You'll still have him when the Crawfords are in town."

"When do you need my answer?"

"Tomorrow. We take off on a two-week road trip the day after."

"Okay. I'll let you know."

"We'd love to have him," said Cool Papa, "but we'll honor your wishes."

I wake up, look at my alarm clock. 2:18 in the morning. What's that noise? Seems to be coming from the kitchen. I see the light's on as well. I walk on tiptoe and nudge open the door. It's my Mama, sitting at the kitchen table, with a cup of coffee. She's holding a framed photo of me and my dad at Kennywood Park Fun Zone, riding the "Wacky Wheel." She's crying.

"What's wrong, Mama?" She puts the picture down, reaches out and hugs me – a long, hard squeeze. She's snuffling right next to my ear. She finally lets me go and I sit next to her.

"I love you, son."

"I know, Mama."

"If your father were here...if he hadn't gotten typhoid..."

"I know. Things would be different."

"I could be at home, looking after you. That's how it should be. That's how we thought it would be."

"I know. I'm sorry."

She finally wipes her eyes, takes my hands and looks at me. "If I let you take this job..."

My heart begins thumping. "Yes, Mama?"

"IF I let you go with Josh and Cool Papa, do you promise to take care of yourself? Pay attention at all times? No daydreaming?"

"No daydreaming, not ever. I've learned my lesson!"

"Do you promise to stay close to Josh? Do your reading and your numbers? And write me a letter every single week, two pages at least, without fail? And to tell me what's really going on in that letter?"

"I will, Mama!"

She looks at me, snuffling, then pulls me into another hug. "I must be crazy."

"No! It's gonna be alright."

"I take Josh at his word that he'll look after you."

"He will!"

"So…IF you promise to pay attention…and write to me every single week…and take care of yourself…"

"I will! I mean, I do! Promise! Cross my heart!"

"Then…oh, Lord help me…we'll give it a try."

And *that's* how I found myself in Scofield, Alabama two weeks later for a game with another white all-star team. And that's where this whole adventure really begins.

CHAPTER FIVE

October 8, 1937

"*Dear Mama,*

How are you? I am fine. You will be happy with the way things are going here. You will be ESPECIALLY happy with the five dollars cash money that's in this envelope, courtesy of my friend Mister Satchel Paige.

I have now been the official batboy of the Pittsburgh Crawfords for going-on two weeks. I know you were worried that I was going to get into trouble because I had too much time on my hands. All I can say is, 'Not hardly.' I've never worked so much in my life

I thought I'd have to work one game a day. Well, guess what? When the Crawfords barnstorm on the road, they usually play two games a day, in two different towns. Sometimes the team even plays what they call a "twilighter" – a third game that begins in the late afternoon and only gets called when it's so dark that neither team can see the ball!

And I'm not just the batboy for the team. I also lug the equipment bags from the bus to the locker room, and from the locker room to the hotel. I fetch the paper bags filled with fried catfish, hamburgers, and egg salad sandwiches from the greasy spoon diners and cafes. I tote the players' uniforms to the local washerwoman Then I wait while she cleans 'em up, and then carry 'em in a duffel bag back to the ballpark.

So where did the five dollars come from? Besides all my other duties, I have become the part-time personal valet for Mister Satchel Paige, which is both a blessing and a curse. The blessing is that he gives dollar tips. The curse is what I have to do to earn the tips. Most of the players have two bags – their baseball gear, and their personal stuff. Satchel has a whole 'nother definition of "things." For Satchel, "things" means a massive steamer trunk filled with his twenty silk suits and 10 pairs of spectator shoes. Then he's got another steamer trunk filled with his shotguns and fishing gear, and a third steamer trunk with his portable typewriter, record player, cameras, ukulele, and medicinal remedies to keep his arm limber and stomach settled. Day before yesterday it got to be too much. I worked three games, and we didn't get to the hotel till midnight. Satchel was yelling for his third trunk and I couldn't budge it. Luckily, I got Mister Deacon Powell on my side. You'd like him, Mama. The Deacon is 6 feet, 5 inches of Biblical righteousness, ready to witness for the downtrodden – in this case, me.

"Satchel," said the Deacon in his deep, melodious preacher-man voice, "The Lord helps those that help themselves. Have mercy on Peanut here, and you'll get your reward in the hereafter." Satchel laughed and came down and helped me...but he didn't tip me. That's okay.

Today feels like a vacation day. We got one game – the Crawfords against the Dizzy Dean Major League All-Stars. Everybody's very excited about this game for a reason I can't tell you about. Anyway, everything's copacetic here. I read the Bible with Cool Papa every night and figure the team averages every morning.

I love you, Mama.

Love, Peanut.

The Crawfords players are excited because Cool Papa Bell told them what was at stake. Cool Papa is friends with a New York sportswriter named Toby Dakota, who works for a paper that is pushing for the integration of major league baseball. Dakota has invited Mister Slatz Randall to the game. Randall is a part-time scout for the Washington Senators, just about the saddest team in the major leagues.

Toby Dakota and Slatz Randall are in the first row behind the dugout, and sometimes I can hear what they're saying. Through the first eight innings, Toby Dakota has done most of the talking about how the Crawfords would "transform" the Senators – make 'em so strong they could beat the Yankees. Now it's the top of the 9th inning, score tied 0 to 0, and Josh is at bat. So far he's had a rough game – two strikeouts and ground ball comebacker to Dizzy.

"He's the only player ever to hit a fair ball clean out of Yankee Stadium," says Toby.

"So I've heard," says Randall, sounding skeptical. "Five times. By you. Like to see what he's got with my own eyes."

Josh steps into the batter's box, and I get goose pimples just watching him get settled. A lot of players have a nervous routine when they step in – they scratch their feet in the dirt, pump the bat, flex their knees, stuff like that. Not Josh. Josh steps into the box, plants his right foot and then his left. Then he rolls up his left sleeve to show off the biggest knot of home run muscle in baseball, and glares at the pitcher. That's it. No pumping, no scratching, no flexing. He doesn't even blink an eye. He doesn't look nervous 'cause he ain't nervous, and that most always makes the pitcher especially nervous.

Dizzy Dean has pitched a hell of a game to this point, but I can see the salty sweat ring on the bill of his St. Louis Cardinals ball cap – he's got to be getting' tired. He fires the first pitch – low and outside. "Stee-rike one!" shouts the umpire. Josh backs out of the box, looking annoyed.

"Weren't even close," he says without turning around. The umpire is a crotchety white man. He's been helping Dizzy's team all day.

"Don't mess with me, boy. Just step in," the umpire snarls. Josh steps in – right foot, left foot, left sleeve, glare at the pitcher. Dizzy unleashes a curve ball that bounces in front of the plate. "Stee-rike two!" Now Josh backs out of the box and turns to the ump. Before he can say anything, the ump whips off his mask and walks right up to him, aiming a finger like a pistol barrel at Josh's nose. "I'm hot, and I'm tired, and I'm ready for this rumpus to be over so I can have an ice cold beer. Best not challenge me, BOY." That last word booms like the sudden bark of a rabid dog. Josh doesn't say a word, but doesn't back off. The ump turns up the lapel of his coat. The sun glints off the gaudy brass pin that reads "KKK." Yikes! The guy's in the Klan! No wonder he's got it in for our guys.

Josh plants his right foot back in the box when another voice splits the air. "Hey, Rastus." Everyone looks toward Mickey Parnell, their big first baseman. "You and the rest o' the coons want to take a watermelon break?" I catch Josh's look. He always looks kind of serious up there, but now – well, if looks could kill, Dizzy Dean would be pushin' up daisies.

"Time!" Dean calls to the umpire, who pulls off his mask.

"Time! Make it snappy, Diz," barks the ump. Dizzy Dean spits a brown rope of tobacco juice into the ground as he trots toward first base. Cool Papa Bell joins me on the top step of the dugout. We have a perfect view of what's coming up. Mickey Parnell is still smiling as Diz grabs a fistful of his uniform shirt.

"C'mon , Diz, I'm trying to rattle him," says Parnell.

"Yeah?" says Dean, taking off his glove. Before Parnell can get his hands up, Diz decks him with his left hand. One punch, KA-BOOM! Then Dizzy spins and heads back to the mound, leaving Parnell to struggle to his feet.

Cool Papa chuckles and says, softly, "Another victory for racial tolerance."

Josh is all focused rage as he faces down the ace right-hander of the National League. A long moment. Everybody's staring at the field. This is it. Dizzy winds up, rears back, and grunts loudly as he fires a fearsome heater on the outside part of the plate. Josh uncoils his upper torso. CRACK!

It's not a sound other hitters make, even home run hitters. That's "horsehide meets hickory," you can hear it in every park and sandlot in America. *This* sound is like the first crack of thunder during a rainstorm – the one that makes you jump three feet in the air. Ducky Medwick, the All-Stars left fielder, doesn't even run toward the fence. He just turns and watches the ball as it disappears over the fence, still zooming skyward. Then, as one, the fans – all of them, black and white – are on their feet. The black fans are cheering. The white fans are staring, mouths open. Everything they've heard – it's all true.

As Josh takes his victory lap around the bases, I can hear Toby Dakota and Mister Slatz Randall right above me. "Well?" says Toby.

"Urrggh..." says Randall, making a choking sound.

"Are you okay?" asks Toby.

"I...I swallowed my chaw," says Randall.

"Here, drink some of this root beer. Didn't I tell you? Didn't I?"

"I been around baseball for 53 years," says Randall. "I seen 'em all. Cap Anson, Honus Wagner, Ty Cobb, and yeah, I even seen the Babe call his shot at the '32 All-Star game. But I ain't NEVER seen NOBODY hit a ball like that."

So now it's one to nothing Crawfords, bottom of the ninth. Satchel strikes out Beau Bell on three pitches, and gets Gee Walker on a dinky fly ball to Cool Papa in center field. And then, like the great showman he is, he decides to send the fans home with souvenir – a memory of the time that the Great Satchel Paige came to Scofield, Alabama and worked his magic. "HEY, DIZ!" Dizzy comes out of the dugout.

"Yeah, Satch?"

"When is Master Mickey Parnell scheduled to bat?"

"He's fourth in the order. Three more guys, then him." Of course, Satch is well aware when Parnell is up. He wants the fans to *know* that he knows.

Now Satch proceeds to give intentional walks – 12 straight wide ones to Josh – to the next three hitters – Rip Radcliff, Flea Clifton, and Chubby Dean. Bags loaded, and here comes Mickey Parnell. Parnell has an ugly purple welt on his jaw, and it matches his mood. He looks like a hornet after somebody whacked the nest. Satch lets him dig in at the plate. Then he steps back off the rubber and yells, "Time!" Parnell backs out as Satch turns to his fielders. "COME ON IN, FELLAS!" I watch Parnell's face crumple into a mask of hatred as all three Crawfords outfielders – Cool Papa Bell, Booker Samuels, and Bullet Hampton – trot in. Once they're on the grassy part of the infielder, Satchel raises both arms in the air and then lowers them, like a preacher lettin' the congregation know it's time to give it a rest in the pews. Seven Crawfords – outfielders and infielders – plop down cross-legged. Then Satch turns back to home plate. Mickey Parnell's face is red as a stop sign. The team's other pitcher, Bullet Hampton, says, "Looks like Satchel wants a little payback."

"You think you can strike me out? Ain't one of your kind alive can strike me out!" shouts Parnell, loud enough for the crowd to hear. This sends Satch and Josh into one of their best routines.

"What'd he say?" asks Satch, cupping his hand to his ear.

"He says he wants a fastball, letter high!" says Josh.

"Fastball, letter high. Got it!" answers Satch. He goes into his most elaborate windup – a triple windmill, with the hesitation at the top, and then smokes a hellacious fastball, letter high, outside part of the plate. Powell takes a mammoth cut and whiffs. He steps out and says to Josh, "Okay, so the porch monkey threw a lucky pitch..."

"What was that?" asks Satch, stepping toward the batter's box.

"He wants a curve ball, inside corner," says Josh.

"Curve ball, inside corner. I aim to please," says Satch. All the Crawfords sitting around the infield are smiling now, which makes Mickey Parnell all the madder. Satch windmills once and then throws his "rainbow pitch" – a big, swooping curve ball that starts at the batter's head, then ducks down and nips the inside part of the plate. Another swing, another miss. As Josh stands to chuck the ball back to Satch, he says, "My, my, my. The full flower of righteous Southern manhood getting' blown away by an uppity colored man." Powell turns to the umpire.

"Can he talk to me like that?" asks Mickey. The umpire just wants this humiliation to end.

"You want to shut him up? Do it with your bat. Get back in the damn box and let's get this megillah over with."

"You got one pitch left, Mickey. Last pitch o' the game. Where you want it?" asks Satch, very politely.

"Just throw the damn ball, you jig." Now, if that were me, I wouldn't go outta my way to make Satch angry. Satch stares at him, and then starts walking toward home plate. He takes off his glove, reaches into his back pocket and pulls out a stick of chewing gum in a silver wrapper. "What's this about?" asks Parnell, but all Satch does is pop the chewing gum in his mouth, and then fold the shiny wrapper until it's the shape of a toothpick. Then he lays the wrapper on the inside black part of the plate. He says to the umpire, "That's your new home plate, right there. That's all I need." He looks at Parnell. "Bee ball. Inside corner. Knee high." Then Satch walks slowly back to the mound.

"What the hell is a 'bee ball'?" asks Parnell, stepping into the box.

"Can't see it. Only hear it buzz by you," answers Josh. "Then it stings your ass."

This is what the crowd has come to see – not a game, but a nail-biting dramatic spectacle, presented as advertised. This is the whole show, right here. This is baseball. Unstoppable force meets immovable object. Fireballing pitcher versus home-run hitting slugger. Satchel windmills twice, kicks his highest kick yet, and turns his entire body into an awesome catapult, whipping an aspirin tablet toward home plate. Powell grunts as he takes an epic cut...but the only crack is the ball exploding in Josh's mitt. The ballpark explodes, every bit of tension erupting in a satisfying roar. Satch just smiles. This is what a great showman does, after all. He makes the biggest possible boast, and then he backs it up 100%. He bows to the Crawfords seated around the infield, and they bow back to him.

Now it's my time to go to work – round up the equipment and get it tucked in the travel bags. I start out on the field, but Deacon Powell grabs me. The long, lean shortstop with the basset hound face shushes me with a finger to his lips. Did I do something wrong? The Deacon points at Toby Dakota and Slatz Randall at the exact moment that Toby hands Slatz over to Cool Papa. Cool Papa smiles as Randall writes something on the back of a business card.

"Wow!" I say to the Deacon. "You really think that he'd..."

"I do indeed, Peanut," says the Deacon. "I believe the Lord works in strange and wondrous ways. I believe that, through his grace, Satch and Josh are finally going get a real tryout. We all know they're good enough to play big league ball. Maybe, finally, the Senators are desperate enough to give our fellas an honest shot." I look at the Deacon, as he looks off toward the field, and then he starts cryin'. Not bawlin' like a baby, just kinda misty-eyed with tears rollin' down his face. He's 37, and – as he puts it – "on the far side of the mountain" as far as his career is concerned. This is the chance he always wanted, but never got. But he ain't bitter. These are tears of joys – for Satch and Josh in particular, and for Negro people overall.

A moment later I'm finally doin' my duty gathering up all the gear and packing it into the bags when I hear a man clearing his throat. "Excuse me, young Sir." I turn around and take in a very peculiar sight – a slender, copper-skinned man in the snappiest double breasted ice-cream suit I ever saw, with a high-style cream colored Borsalino hat and ox-blood red and white spectator shoes. He looks like a Hollywood star in one of those newsreel films, arriving in Europe for a movie premiere.

"Yeah?" I stutter. What does he want with me?

"My name is Dr. Enrique Aybar." He bends down to shake my hand. His hand is soft. This guy isn't a ballplayer. "The Negro players – you work for them, yes?" He's from some other place than America, but I can't quite tell where. Mexico? Cuba?

"I'm the equipment manager," I tell him, because I have successfully proven I am more than a mere 'batboy.'

"Just so," he says. "Would you be willing to perform a small kindness for me?"

"Depends." What does this guy want? An autographed baseball? Seats behind home plate for the next game? He reaches into his inside breast pocket and hands me his business card, wrapped in a five-dollar bill. More money for Mama. I pocket the nickel note and read the card:

Dr. Jose Enrique Aybar
Dean, University of Santo Domingo
Deputy, National Congress of the Dominican Republic
Director of Baseball Operations,
Ciudad Trujillo Dragones

Hmmmm. I don't know what to make of this. Does he want the Crawfords to play the "Dragones" in an exhibition game?

"I wish to speak to Señor Paige. About engaging his services, and perhaps those of his fellows."

"This team of yours – the 'Dragones' – you want them to play the Crawfords?"

"Not exactly. It would be best if I could speak to Señor Paige personally." Before I can ask another question, he raises his hand. "Please. I have traveled a very long distance. Will you do me this favor? Give him this card, tell him I wish a moment of his time?" I nod that I will. He gives a small bow of thanks, then spins and walks off. I haul the last bag of gear into the dugout when Booker Samuels runs up to Cool Papa Bell and says, "Papa, better come quick. Problem with the money." Cool Papa runs off, yelling instructions behind him.

"Get that stuff on the bus and stay there, in case we need to make a getaway."

"'Kay!" I yell. But after I load the stuff on the bus, I slink over to the box office. I want to see what's going on.

CHAPTER SIX

"That's all there is, son. The whole ball of wax in a nutshell. That's the winner's share, as promised." The man sayin' this is Bascomb Crowley, 315 pounds of sweaty, grinning bluster and hoopla seated behind a beat-up desk in the box office. He's rolling a huge glass tumbler of iced tea across his forehead. Standing beside him and holding a mean-looking shotgun in the crook of his arm is Early Patchett, the umpire from the game, and also the Sheriff of Scofield. Cool Papa Bell is on our side of the desk, along with Josh, Satch and Booker Samuels. Bascomb's newspaper, the "Scofield Intelligencer," promoted the game. He staged the boxing match before the game, and introduced Miss Scofield 1937 (by an amazing coincidence, also his daughter) to throw out the first ball. Bascomb puts down the tea and pushes a cigar box full of cash money at Cool Papa, who isn't looking at the money; he's looking right at Bascomb

"Know what pains me the most, Mister Crowley?" says Cool Papa.

"What's that, boy?" says the fat man. I guess he doesn't notice that Cool Papa is about the same age he is.

"What pains me the most is that you think I'm simpleminded. Why do you take me for a fool?"

"I don't, uh, think, uhhhh..." Cool Papa leans in toward Bascomb's flushed face.

"You don't think I'm smart enough to post one of our boys across from the box office? Countin' the customers? Booker, tell him what you told me." Booker Samuels, the Crawfords' whip-smart 27-year-old right fielder, steps forward. "Booker here has a Bachelor of Science in Business Administration from the Tuskegee Institute." Booker consults a small spiral bound notebook as he speaks.

"From 11:35 to 1:15 p.m. when it shut down, the box office sold 1,123 adult tickets at 50 cents a ticket, and 708 kids' tickets at 10 cents at ticket, for a grand total of 632 dollars and 50 cents." Booker looks up from his notebook and fixes Mr. Crowley with a disdainful glare. "Half of that minus 10% for expenses – that would be what you promised, the winner's share – is 284 dollars and 63 cents."

"And yet what have we got here in the box?" asks Cool Papa. "120 dollars. That's not even half what we're owed." Bascomb never stops smiling.

"Well, I think you boys misremembered our agreement. Plus expenses ran a little higher than we expected. Right, Sheriff?" The Sheriff gives a single nod. "Ask me," says Bascomb, "This is pretty good money for some colored boys playing a sandlot game in the middle of the afternoon in Alabama. Couldn't make nearly this much sweatin' in a cotton field." Cool Papa looks at Josh, who looks at Satch, who looks at the shotgun. I catch a look on Josh's face that reminds me of my father, when he was being pushed around by a bully. Actually, it was a series of looks, all in a row – anger, disgust, hopelessness, and resignation. Cool Papa wearily picks up the cash and hands it to Booker, who puts it in the team cash box. Bascomb smiles his biggest smile yet and says, "You boys were a damn good attraction. Y'all come back next year."

"Not sure we can afford to," says Josh.

Basomb jiggles as he laughs. "The Sheriff here will make sure you boys get out of town safely."

As we trudge to the bus, we hear a shout. "SATCH! JOSH!" Everyone turns and sees Toby Dakota with Mister Slatz Randall. "Hey fellas, here's that Scout I mentioned." Toby fades into the background as the Scout hands Satch his business card.

Norval "Slatz" Randall
Special Scout – Alabama, Georgia, Mississippi
Washington Senators Baseball Club

Cool Papa reaches out his hand, but before he can say anything, Satch says, "'Bout goddamn time!" Now, I don't know much about what my mama calls "proper social etiquette," but cursing a white man who wants to do you a favor seems like a bad idea. Luckily, Mr. Randall laughs.

"Heck of a ballgame, Satch. 'Specially your little show there at the end."

"Weren't no show," says Satch. "A show is something made up. What I did was the real deal," says Satch. "Now tell us why you're here. As if we didn't know."

"Mr. Griffith would like..."

"We KNOW what Mister Calvin Griffith would like," interrupts Satch. "He would like to win some damn ballgames, which he's never gonna do with that bunch of humpty-dumptys he's got out there now. That team is PATHETIC." I'm afraid Satch is going to rile Mr. Randall, but he just chuckles.

"They are a pretty sad bunch," says Randall. Now Josh steps forward.

"Does this mean that we get a tryout? A real shot at playin' for the Senators?"

"All Mr. Griffith told me on the telephone just now," says Randall, "Is that he...let's see, how did he put it...he wants to meet you, because he wants to 'make a little history.'" Satch turns to Josh and nods his head and then turns to Randall.

"If Mr. Griffith puts Satchel Paige, Josh Gibson and Cool Papa Bell on the Washington Senators, he'll do more than make history. He'll make himself rich, make himself happy, and make himself the friend of every black person in America, because he'll make himself the owner of the best baseball team in the world. And that ain't braggin'. That's just a natural fact."

"I believe you boys can do it, but I ain't makin' no promises, 'cept one. I'll set up a meeting with Mr. Griffith."

"We'll be there," says Josh.

At that moment, it hits me – I just might be the batboy for the Washington Senators next season! In the major leagues! On a team that wins the pennant, and then the World Series! Suddenly my head is filled with visions of flash bulbs popping, fifty thousand fans screaming their lungs out, pennants waving, fireworks going off, and suddenly I'm sitting in back of a Packard convertible the size of a battleship, cruising down a street in New York getting smothered in ticker tape, just like when a war ends or some aviator breaks a speed record for flying around the world. And there I am, shakin' the hand of Mister Franklin Delano Roosevelt in the White House as he presents us with our World Series trophy!

"PEANUT!" Suddenly I snap back into the real world. "You put the stuff in the bus like I asked?" says Cool Papa.

"You bet I did."

"Then let's get outta here."

"You bet." So much for shakin' FDR's hand. I gotta figure out how to slip away, find a pay phone and tell Mister Gus Greenlee that it ain't just Satchel. All three of his best players might jump clear out of the Negro National League to the Washington Senators.

You want to know what its like to travel with the Pittsburgh Crawfords? Then you have to know what it's like to bobble along hundreds of miles on a rickety bus on bumpy back dirt roads. Everybody's still in their dirty uniforms because the ballpark had showers but colored players were forbidden by law to use them, and the bus smells like whatever is left over in the bags of trash from our last meal stop. Cool Papa is the bus driver and he does his best, but just when you get settled into a nice comfortable doze, you hit a big ol' rut, and...

"Hey!" yells Satch.

"Sorry, fellas," says Cool Papa.

"Oh, man! You bumped me outta my dream! Satchel was dreamin' 'bout life in the big leagues."

"And what's that going to be like?" asks Booker. Satch's smile is blissful.

"Big paydays. Jam-packed ballparks. Front page stories with a picture of my handsome face in every sports section in America. Clean locker rooms with hot showers. And best of all, no damn busses. Trains only. Pullman cars with feather beds. Colored brother picks up your jive and carries it for you, and says 'Thank you, Sir' when you hand him that dollar tip."

"Hey, Peanut does that already," says Payday Thompson

"Best of all," adds Josh, "don't have to worry about bein' cheated out what you worked for."

"Work *half* the year, April to October, and the rest of the year I'm fishin'," said Satch. "First class all the way."

"Speaking of first class, where we stayin' tonight?" says Josh.

"The Elite Hotel," says Cool Papa Bell as he wrestles the bus's steering wheel, as big as a manhole cover. "Real indoor plumbing and a shower on every floor." Josh smiles at me.

"Man, it's been five days since I slept in a real hotel bed with nice crispy white sheets."

I can tell we're in big trouble the second we pull up in front of the Elite Hotel. It's the shingle that hangs underneath that sign that gives it away – "Under New Management – No Coloreds." Now I'm standing at the front desk listening to Cool Papa tangle with the desk clerk. She's a mean white lady in her early 20's who stares at us like we're escaped convicts.

"We have a reservation," says Booker.

"It's not here," says the woman, putting her hand on the beat-up reservations ledger."

"You didn't even check your book."

"I don't have to."

"We put down a deposit."

"My daddy returned all the deposits from colored folk when he bought this hotel." A white couple walk past us, and shoot the clerk a dirty look. This gal wants us to disappear. This is bad. "If you don't leave right now," she says in a whisper, "I'm gonna call the Sheriff."

"Okay, look," says Cool Papa. "We been on the road for five hours. The guys are hungry. I see you got a dining room. How 'bout letting us grab a meal?"

"Our dining room don't allow no coloreds neither," she hisses.

"Put some sandwiches in a bag, we'll take 'em to go."

"We can't sell no food to no coloreds," she says. A smiling Deacon Powell steps forward, and uses his "Sunday sermon baritone."

"What if we were to produce a peerless paragon of lily-white Southern manhood to purchase said sandwiches? I'm certain that would quell your qualms." Yeah, the Deacon really talks like that. It just seems to make the clerk angrier.

"I believe we just ran out of sandwiches. Now you boys GIT," she snarls. Josh steps forward. He's almost a foot taller than she is, and she shrinks as he towers over her.

"How 'bout this. I saw you got a well behind this place. Can we at least bring a bucket up and have us a drink of your water?"

"Can't do that." Her face is fixed in an angry grimace.

"Why not?"

"If folks 'round here heard that coloreds drank from our well, we'd have to shut it down permanent. That's all I'm gonna take of this. I'm callin' the Sheriff right now." She comes out from behind the desk and makes a beeline for the telephone on the opposite wall. We all try to get out of her way, but I bump into Deacon Powell, who knocks over Cool Papa. She runs straight into me, landing on top of me as we both tumble to the floor. She screams as she pushes off me like I had smallpox or something. "Get out! GET OUT! HELP! PLEASE HELP ME! SOMEBODY HELP ME, PLEASE!" She's hysterical. Nothing good can come of this. We high-tail it out of that place, jump back on the bus and rumble off as fast as we can.

As the last lights of the town disappear in the rear window, Cool Papa Bell delivers the bad news. "Gentlemen, he says, "we are goin' camping." The collective groan rattles the windows of the bus.

CHAPTER SEVEN

After all that mess we need a piece of luck. Deacon Powell has taken over the driving chores. He chunks the bus down that rutted road as we all rubberneck out the window looking for just the right camping spot – open enough to pitch the tents and woodsy enough to give us some cover in case it rains. We get our piece of luck when Deacon shouts out, "And on that most *glorious* day, oh Lord, we shall *praise thee* as our *salvation*, for thou hast *answered our prayers* and delivered your wandering children of Israel to the campground of *thy most beloved and exalted Disciple of Hi-De-Ho, Mister Cab Calloway!*"

All eyes swivel to the right-side windows. We see a campground that is already set up, with 15 or so fellas in residence. Their bus is painted top to bottom with a huge sign that says, "Cab Calloway And His Famous Cotton Club Orchestra! Join the Jitterbug Party with the Harlem's Hi-De-Ho Man!" The Deacon opens the door and Cab Calloway himself hops in to greet us. "Greetings, gates! I'm guessin' you got the same chilly howdy-do we got back there in town, but it don't make no difference no how, 'cuz we got ourselves a mighty fine party right here under the stars." All the Crawfords know Cab, and he knows us because the Calloway band plays the Crawford Grille when Cab's not up in Harlem at the Cotton Club.

I can tell right away this is going to be one of the busiest nights I ever spent. It's one thing to tote all the baseball gear from the bus to the dugout, but tonight I have to unload all this camping gear that I didn't even know was on the bus – canvas tents, cooking stoves, blankets, gas lanterns, and of course all of Satchel's fishing and hunting gear. Everybody helps out, and before I know it I'm sitting in front of a campfire with a pretty good plate of hobo stew, taking in the scene. And what a scene:

There's Calloway's best players – Doc Cheatam, DePriest Wheeler, and Chauncey Haughton – havin' a fine jam session. They're riffing on "I've Got My Love to Keep Me Warm." Three of the Crawfords – Flash Fowler, Deacon Powell and Bullet Hampton – are harmonizing on the chorus.

There's Keg Johnson, Calloway's ace trombone player, lecturing Cool Papa Bell on the "art" of making hobo stew. "Now this here stew," says Johnson, "is a dynamic combustion of the stuff we brought – cans of peas, lima beans, and tomatoes – the stuff we dug up in a field – potatoes, beets, and radishes – and the stuff we just shot in these here woods – rabbits and possums. You always want more rabbits than possums, but if you got enough Worcestershire sauce, red pepper, and vinegar it don't make no difference no how. And if all else fails, add more catsup."

There's Mister Cab Calloway, looking very dapper in his pearl gray sweatshirt, pleated suit pants and fancy suede shoes, chattin' up Cool Papa, Josh and Satchel about who is the best player in the world. Cab is thumbing through the new copy of "Colored Baseball and Sports Monthly" magazine. "Now according to this here article by a Mister Fletcher O'Dell, Senior Sportswriter for the *Pittsburgh Courier*," says Cab, "the two greatest ballplayers in the world are Satchel Paige, the sepia cyclone and virtually unhittable when he's on his game...."

"Damn straight," says Satch, as Cab chortles and continues.

"...and Josh Gibson, the black Babe Ruth, whose very presence in the batter's box is enough to give pitchers the galloping heebie-jeebies."

"Sounds 'bout right," says Josh.

"Does he say who is better?" I ask.

"Does not," replies Cab. "It does, however, quote Mister Satchel Paige as saying...." He thumbs several pages to find the quote. "I can strike out any batter in baseball..."

"Anytime, anywhere." Satch finishes the sentence. Cab smiles at Satch.

"You stand by those words?"

"Satchel Paige says what he means, and means what he says." Now Cab turns to Josh.

"Joshua, you have an opinion about that bit of bravado?" Josh is staring at Satch. No hatred in the stare, more like sizing him up.

"Strike me out? Whenever he wants? Ain't no days like that."

"You can hit him? On his best day? That what you're sayin'?" asks Cab. Josh looks toward Cab.

"Yeah. That's what I'm sayin'."

"Wellllllllllllll now," says a smiling Cab Calloway. "We got us a nice little pea patch here, and two busses with working headlights. What would you cats say to settling this squabble right here and right now?" What? Does Cab really mean it?

"Suits me," says Josh.

"Sounds good," says Satch. And suddenly the game is on.

Cool Papa and Cab turn the busses around so they throw light on our makeshift field. I drag out two bags of baseball gear. Chu Berry, Cab's stellar tenor sax man, paces off the sixty feet six inches between where Satch is gonna stand (marked by one of Cab's over-sized bandleader batons) and home plate (a cymbal from LeRoy Maxie's drum kit). A gleeful Payday Thompson is taking bets, with Satch a 3-2 favorite to strike Josh out, heavy action on both players.

"Last call, everybody! Get 'em down!" Satch sidles up and hands Payday a ten dollar bill. "Dime note on Mister Satchel Paige, if you please. Sorry, it's all I got." Not to be outdone, Josh comes up and hands him a ten-spot as well. "When you pay me off, be sure and include Satch's sawbuck in the kitty. Make it all the sweeter."

Josh can't catch because he's hittin', so Booker Samuels puts on the "tools of ignorance" and sets up behind home plate. And the umpire? The only man that both Satch and Josh can agree on is Mister Cab Calloway himself, who is delighted to be part of the action. Cab lays out the ground rules. "This is just like reg'lar baseball, friends. One at bat. For Satchel to win the bet, he has to strike out Josh – not on three pitches, just whiff him fair and square. For Josh to win, he has to put hickory to horsehide, in something that can reasonably be called fair territory. If he wants to show off and hit one of those legendary home runs, let's call that the maraschino cherry on the banana split – real nice, but not essential to declare victory."

Players and band members form up in two lines on either side of the action. Payday Thompson takes bets right up to the moment Satch rears back and fires the first pitch – a high and inside "headhunter" meant to scare the daylights out of Josh. All Josh does is bend back and let the pitch pass about a half inch from his face. Man, he is one cool customer. "Ball one!" cries Cab. Now Satch goes into a double windmill and throws a big rainbow curveball that just nips the outside of the plate. Josh never moves.

"Steeee-rike one!" shouts Cab. Everyone starts to quiet down now – this is getting serious. Even Satch, who loves to chat up the batter after every pitch, is mute. This ain't every batter. This is Josh Gibson, and Satch's reputation is on the line.

Satch goes into a *triple* windmill, and fires his best "bee ball," low and inside. Josh takes a rip, foul tipping it into Booker's mask. The ball is travelin' so fast it knocks Booker back into Cab, and they both go down like bowling pins. "Stee-rike two!" shouts Cab, as he and Booker help each other get upright.

Now the assembled gawkers are dead quiet. They know they are watchin' history. Just as Satch is ready to start his windup, Payday Thompson yells, "Last chance for action on this!" and we have to take a two minute break while the very last bets are placed. "Play ball!" hollers Cab.

Satch tries to stare down Josh, who rolls up his left sleeve to show off that massive knot of muscle. Then Josh anchors his right foot in the box, plants his left foot, and returns Satch's no-blink stare. I've never seen Satch be so still – just lookin' at Josh. Now guys aren't just quiet – we're all holding our breath.

Satch raises his arms over his head, starts to windmill, and then freezes, paralyzed by the fierce glare of wigwagging light beams. What's happening? The sky has exploded with ten billion fireflies, right out of nowhere! I whirl around. A whole bunch of beat up Model A Fords have skidded up and surrounded us on both sides. The headlights are blinding us, but I move so's I can see what this is about. The doors open, and I choke as my throat closes. Oh no! 25 silvery-white Ku Klux Klan robes, complete with pointy-white hats are coming at us. The hands poking out of those robes are holding shotguns. I whirl around – they're coming at us from every direction. I back up and bump into Josh.

One of the Kluxers steps forward. He's holding a thick coil of brown rope that ends in a big fat noose. "Which one o' you boys laid your filthy hands on my Ellie?" So that's it. This is the daddy of the hotel clerk – the one I bumped into. The blood drains out of my face and I feel like I'm going to throw up. Two minutes ago I was watching the greatest baseball matchup in history. Seems like two years ago. I swallow hard, and start to take a step forward. Then an iron hand crushes my shoulder, and I freeze in place. Josh. He steps in front of me, and walks right up to the Imperial Wizard.

"That'd be me," he says. I open my mouth to protest, but nothing comes out. My mouth is bone dry – I can't even whisper. *This is the second time he's saved my life.* The Klan members take a step toward Josh. He takes a big stride toward them holding that huge bat, and they stutter-step backwards. The rest of the fellas see what's happenin' – the Kluxers are actually scared of Josh, even though they're the ones holding shotguns.

"Get him! Get the big gorilla!" yells the Wizard, and some of his playmates start edging toward Josh, but not so close that Josh can nail 'em with his war club.

"Well c'mon. I'm right here. Come and get me," says Josh. Three Kluxers charge him from behind. Josh whirls around, swings, and catches one of them in the side of the head. The crack is sickening, and the guy lurches sideways and falls in a heap, moaning as his Klan cowl turns crimson. Nobody helps him.

"You believe in God, son?" The Deacon has moved in behind me.

"I…ummm…."

"Just say yes."

"Yeah, sort of. I guess," I say.

"Good enough. Then let's you and me ask him to bring down a miracle, right now."

The Kluxers are moving in on Josh little by little, and I know he can't hold out much longer. Two of 'em have their guns trained on our fellas to keep us from helping Josh. Suddenly, three of them rush Josh. He swings the bat, but one of the Kluxers blocks it with his shotgun, which snaps the bat at the handle. Now they grab him and throw him on the ground, and it takes seven of them to hold him there. Reminds me of a picture I saw in a storybook of the little folks holding down Gulliver in Lilliput. "HA! Gotcha!" The Wizard kneels down and slips the noose over Josh's head and tightens it around his neck. Then his boys stand Josh up. His buddies have found a "lynchin' tree" with a strong branch just far enough off the ground. The seven members march Josh over to the tree. The Wizard tosses the pullin' end of the rope over the branch. One of his flunkies has fetched a Brownie camera, and positions himself so he can capture the big moment.

"Please, God, please," I whisper to myself. "Never asked for nothin' before this, but please help Josh. He's a good man, he's my friend. Do something, just this once, please..."

KA-BOOM! A rifle shot rings out and echoes off the trees. Everyone looks at everyone else, and then every eye settles on the Wizard, who is spinning around, a red splotch blooming at his right shoulder. His eyes widen, like he can't believe what just happened to him. He drops the rope, and falls over backwards.

And then all hell breaks loose.

The Kluxers are panicked. They whirl like dervishes, their silvery robes catching the headlights as they try to figure out where that shot came from. KA-BOOM! Another rifle shot shatters the limb of the hanging tree, and the Kluxers start running into each other as they look for cover. Josh has freed himself from the noose. He picks up a huge tree branch and goes after the lynch mob. As he passes me, he says, "Satchel's got some shotguns. Get 'em." I scurry to the bus, zigzagging through this battlefield. Two other KKKers are duking it out with Bullet Hampton and Chauncey Haughton, Calloway's clarinet player.

I race onto the bus and rummage through the gear until I find the shotguns. Dang! Not loaded. I dig out his shells, and load 'em just like my daddy showed me. I race off the bus just in time to see Josh fighting off two Kluxers, only he can't see a third one picking up a shotgun and taking a bead on this chest. "Josh!" I scream. "Look out!" It's up to me. Can I kill a man, if it saves another man's life? I shiver all over as I drop one rifle and lift the other to my shoulder. And then a sizzling fastball conks that Kluxer square in the back of his noggin, and he goes down face first in the dirt. And there's Satchel, smilin' like the Cheshire Cat. Dang. If he can throw a pitch like that when a man's life is at stake, maybe he CAN strike out Josh.

I dodge a Kluxer as he falls, victim of a wicked body block by Cool Papa. I hand Satch's shotgun to Deacon Powell, who fires both barrels over the heads of the combatants. Now the Kluxers are in full retreat, stumbling for their cars. Our guys stand there watchin' as the Klan guys screech away into the night. The last one to hobble off is the Wizard himself, a blood-soaked wreck yellin' for his guys to come back and fight like men instead of running like cowards.

And then it's over, just like waking up from a bad dream The campground is littered with broken shotguns, tattered Klan hoods and blood-caked baseball bats. After all that racket, the quiet is kind of scary. The guys are checking each other out. Lots of cuts, scrapes, and bruises, but nobody got himself shot up. Josh comes up to me. "You okay, little brother?"

"Yeah. You?"

"Yeah, never better." Satchel comes up to us.

"What I want to know is..."

"Yeah, me too," says Josh. Everyone's looking around. Where did those shots come from? And then the question gets answered. Two figures are coming toward us from the woods.

"Hey," I say as they come closer.

"What?" says Cool Papa.

"I know that guy! He was at the game. Doctor...something." Before I can remember, the two men are in our camp. The Doctor is in the same double-breasted ice cream suit he was wearing in when we met. The other one is a scowling, beetle-browed bear in khaki army fatigues. He's carrying a rifle. The one in the suit comes right over to me.

"Good evening, young Sir! Might I have a word with your friends now?"

"Uhhhh...yeah, sure. I guess. You the fellas that scared off the bedsheet brigade?" He smiles and nods, then reaches his hand out to Satchel.

"Do I have the distinct honor and privilege of addressing the greatest pitcher the game of baseball has ever known, Mister Satchel Paige?" Satchel smiles. Dr. Aybar knows what he's doin'.

"You certainly do," says Satch.

"Dr. Enrique Aybar, Director of Baseball Operations for the national team of the Dominican

Republic." No wonder I couldn't quite place the accent! Aybar presents his business card, and turns to his partner.

"Allow me to introduce Señor Maximo Borgatti, Chief of the Guardia Nacional, Head of the Military Intelligence Service and Personal Security Officer for the Benefactor of our Beloved Fatherland, Dr. Rafael Trujillo." Borgatti glowers at us, still holding the rifle that broke up the Klan's necktie party. Reminds me of a junkyard bulldog one particularly nasty loan shark used to keep back in Pittsburgh to scare his clients into paying on time.

Handshakes all around. Josh says, "Since you followed us all the way up here and saved our lives, I assume you got something pretty important on your mind."

"How 'bout if we chat about this over some hot coffee and hobo stew?" says Cool Papa. And in two jiffies we're back to something like what we had before the Klan crashed the party, 'cept for Payday Thompson and Booker Samuels on guard duty with Satch's shotguns. The stew pot is bubbling, the coffee is percolating, the jam session is back on, and Dr. Aybar is hunkered down with Satch, Josh, and Cool Papa.

"Thanks again for savin' our butts," says Satch.

"And my neck," says Josh, his meaty hand rubbing the burn on his throat. "They woulda lynched me for sure."

"Course, in this life," says Satch, suddenly the businessman, "ain't nobody do nothin' for nobody outta the kindness of their hearts. So what's this all about?"

"Señores," says Aybar, "how would you like a paid vacation in paradise?" Satch and Josh look at each other, and then bust out laughing.

"Come again?" asks Satch. Aybar fixes on him as we all look on.

"Señor Paige, let me speak frankly. Our people – the Dominican people – love three things above all else."

"And what are those three things?" asks Satch.

"The first is baseball. The second is baseball. The third, as I'm sure you can guess is, of course, baseball. You, Señor Paige, are as a god in our homeland. Your feats are whispered about, as those of a storybook character. Players who have faced you come to our country and share tales of your astonishing prowess. They speak of one who transcends the earthly domain of a mere baseball pitcher. You are a sorcerer, able to do things with a baseball no mortal could possibly achieve." What Satch can do with a baseball, this guy can do with words. Satch practically sprains his neck nodding in agreement.

"Gospel truth, every word," says Satchel.

"The Great Benefactor of our Fatherland, Dr. Trujillo, wishes you to share your gifts with our people. He wants to fly you and eight of your hand-picked compatriots to our country, so that you can represent our beloved Dominican national team, the Ciudad Trujillo Dragones in a five game series with our rivals, the San Pedro de Macoris Sugar Kings."

"Five games," says Satch.

"Correct," says Aybar.

"For money," says Satch.

"You will be paid, yes," says Aybar.

"LOTS of money," says Satch.

"Satch, the man just saved our lives!" says Josh.

"And Satchel is most thankful for his efforts, Josh, but life-savin' is one thing and business is somethin' else again." Gus Greenlee couldn't have said it better. No wonder Gus and Satch are always circling each other.

"I believe that what I'm authorized to pay will more than satisfy you," says Aybar. Satchel takes his measure. Not sure anyone has ever agreed to his demands before he's even made them.

"Satchel Paige is the highest paid player in all of baseball. In the world. Including the big leagues." Aybar smiles.

"Just so. This is because you have ascended to the pantheon of baseball gods. That is why our Most Exalted Benefactor wishes you to play for the glory of our country." Josh looks at Aybar. Something fishy here.

"Dr. Aybar," says Josh, "what's this all about? Feels like there's something you're not telling us."

"Why do you think that?" asks Borgatti. First time he's spoken. Nasty edge to the question. Josh eyeballs him. Borgatti returns the look.

"Just a feelin'," says Josh. Aybar breaks the tension.

"Have you ever had a dream, Señor Gibson? I'm sure you have. Dr. Trujillo's dream is to create, as a gift to his people, the mightiest baseball team the Hemisphere has ever known, with the best players in the world."

"Not the best *black* players. The best *players*," says Josh.

"Just so," says Aybar. "The best *players*. Dr. Trujillo believes that, in winning a glorious victory for our country, this team will provide our people with an inspiring, inspirational message – that our destiny as a people is to achieve a victory over whatever forces seek to limit us. You gentlemen will help make Dr. Trujillo's dream – and the dreams of the Dominican people – come true."

Aybar's words hang in the air like those of a preacher man reaching for the stars at the end of a Sunday sermon. He doesn't just want to win some ballgames. He wants to make history! Before Satch can agree, Josh speaks up.

"That's a mighty generous offer. We're gonna have to think it over." Borgatti grunts, spits on the ground and turns to Aybar.

"I knew this was a waste of time." Borgatti turns away, but Aybar holds up a hand, then he smiles at Josh.

"Is there someone else...how to say this...vying for your services?" says Aybar.

"You asked if we have a dream," says Josh. "We do. We want to play in the major leagues – to be the first black men to play major league baseball. We're on our way to Washington, D.C., Mr. Aybar, to see Calvin Griffith. About playing for his team, the Washington Senators." Borgatti takes a step toward Josh and scowls at him. Then, before anyone knows what's happening, he brings up the rifle and points it at Josh's chest,

"We saved your lives, Señor Gibson." Borgatti pauses, then lowers his voice as he taps Josh's heart with the rifle barrel. "I...saved...your...life." They're staring at each other again, neither one breaking it off. After a long moment, Josh grabs the rifle barrel, and pushes it away.

"And I thanked you for doing that," says Josh. More staring. Finally, Dr. Aybar breaks the tension.

"We have come here to *invite* you gentlemen, not to make demands." He pulls out another business card, followed by that fancy fountain pen. He scribbles something on the card, and hands it to Satch. Then he shakes everyone's hand – Satch, Josh, Cool Papa, the Deacon, and even me.

"We will be leaving the day after tomorrow," says Dr. Aybar. "I sincerely hope the Senators provide you the opportunities you seek. If your meeting with Mr. Griffith proves unsatisfactory, meet me at my hotel at this time. I believe all your questions can be answered, and all your desires, monetary and otherwise, can be honored."

"We'll see about that," says Satch.

"If you should accept the Great Benefactor's invitation," says Dr. Aybar "our people will welcome you as the gods of baseball that you are. You will meet your true destiny as players, and as men. Until then..." He gives us a little wave, then turns and walks off toward his car. Señor Borgatti just stands there, scowling at Josh. Something personal between these two, but I have no idea what it is, since they just met. Finally, Borgatti and his rifle turn and march toward Dr. Aybar. Josh stares at him as Deacon Powell puts his big hands on my shoulders.

"That guy is scary," I whisper.

"Be not overcome of evil, but overcome evil with good," says the Deacon.

"Bible?"

"Romans 12:21."

"Easier said than done," I say.

"You got that right," says the Deacon, laughing.

CHAPTER EIGHT

October 9. 1937

What an adventure! Got up at the crack of dawn, snuck away from the hotel and found the pay phone at the Jubilee Diner, where I placed my very first collect call to the Crawford Grille. Mr. Greenlee had just gone to bed, but Mister Bonecrusher Doaks accepted the charges and took a message – Greenlee's three best players had not one but TWO offers to jump the team! I was earning my keep, for sure.

Now we – Satch, Josh, Cool Papa, and myself – are standing just outside the business offices of the Washington Senators Baseball Club, inside Griffith Stadium. We're staring at the golden words etched on the door's beveled glass:

WASHINGTON SENATORS
AMERICAN LEAGUE BASEBALL CLUB
WORLD CHAMPIONS 1924
Clark Griffith, President

"I waited my whole life to get here," says Josh.

"That makes two of us," says Cool Papa.

"Hope they don't ask Satchel to take a pay cut, 'cuz that ain't gonna happen," says Satch, half-joking. He reaches for the doorknob, but Cool Papa holds up both hands to stop him.

"Remember," says Cool Papa, "We're not here to beg them to do anything. We *belong* on that field with them. THEY need US."

Now we're in the lobby. I always dreamed of what this might be like, but the real thing is even better. Ceilings like a cathedral. Shiny marble floors. Photograph after photograph of Presidents shaking hands with ballplayers and Broadway show stars throwing out the first ball. The walls are lined with ritzy glass cases filled with great stuff. There's Walter Johnson's glove, the ball he used in his 1919 no-hitter against the Red Sox, and some bats, including the one Goose Goslin used in the fourth game of the 1924 World Series, where he got four hits and a home run to win the game. In the dead center of the room is a giant glass trophy case that holds four loving cups. The three smaller ones are for winning American League pennants in 1924, 1925 and 1933. They're positioned so they look like they're holding up the biggest and gaudiest loving cup of all– a huge golden cup for winning the World Series in 1924.

A secretary – a stick-like older lady with a thin lipped frown, mousy brown hair in a bun, and glasses on a chain around her neck – watches us like we're gonna steal the paperclips off her desk. Josh doesn't even notice her until he puts his hand on Goose

Goslin's bat. "Please don't touch that," she says. He looks at her. I can see him size her up in a single glance. He considers his options. Yes, he has every right to pick up that bat. No, she probably can't stop him. Yes, it might make her mad and she might tell somebody who might then tell Mr. Griffith. He takes his hand off the bat. "You boys have a reason for being here?" she asks, with just the tiniest nudge in her voice on the word "boys."

"Men. We're men," says Josh quietly.

"We've got a meeting with Mr. Griffith," says Cool Papa, and the Secretary's eyebrows shoot up in shock.

"Mister...Griffith? Mister Clark Griffith?" she says, amazed at the cheek of these colored rascals lying so brazenly. Papa plays it cool and polite.

"That's right, ma'am," says Cool Papa. "We're expected." She picks up her phone and dials her boss like she's calling the police about a burglar coming at her with a pipe wrench.

"Mr. Griffith, there's a group of colored..." She pauses, listens. "They are?" Her face goes pale. She whispers, "Yes, Sir." Two seconds later, Mr. Griffith comes striding out of his office.

"Fellas, glad you came." He shakes everyone's hand, even mine. He's a sharp lookin' older gentleman, skinny with silver hair and eyebrows, wearing a natty three piece gray suit with a gold pocket watch chained to his vest. He says, "Mona, hold my calls" as he herds us into his office.

The office is an even busier version of the waiting room, only this time every picture shows Mr. Griffith himself shaking hands with the big shots – Herbert Hoover, Charles Lindbergh, Clark Gable, and Will Rogers. The glass cases and picture frames show pennants, awards, and scorecards from the Senators' greatest games. Directly behind his desk is a gigantic oil painting of Mr. Griffith shaking hands with the greatest player in team history, the "Big Train" himself, Mister Walter Johnson. They're standing under a huge banner that says "Washington Senators – 1924 Baseball World Champions." A large easel dominates one corner of the room. A white lace curtain is draped over it.

I'm happy, 'cuz everyone else is so excited by bein' here. Satchel tries to hide it, but Josh and Cool Papa are smiling smiles that say, *"We made it, and all the nonsense we put up with was worth it."* They are finally on the carousel, and the big brass ring is there for the grabbing.

"Thanks for coming here, boys," says Mr. Griffith, now settled behind his desk. I see Josh wince at "boys," but he lets it pass.

"We're delighted to be here," says Cool Papa. "I've been trying to set this up for two years."

"Mister Griffith, if you'll give us a chance, sign us up…" says Josh.

"For the right damn price, of course," says Satchel.

"…we can win you the pennant by 10 damn games, guaranteed." Josh's smile fades as we all watch Griffith flinch. It's as if Josh just slapped him in the face.

"Pennant?"

"Yeah," says Josh, puzzled. "That's the idea, right?"

"Why else would you want to sign us?" asks Cool Papa. Griffith is puzzled, like he doesn't understand the question.

"What are we talking about here?" says Griffith. I – none of us, in fact – can understand why he's confused.

"That agent fella said you were interested in signing us up for the Senators," says Cool Papa.

"Who said that?" says Griffith.

"Slatz Randall," says Josh.

"He said I wanted to sign you...for the SENATORS?" says Griffith, clearly horrified.

"Yeah! He said..." Cool Papa pauses, trying to remember his exact words. "What he said was that you were 'interested making some history.'"

"We all heard him say it," I say.

"You did say that, didn't you?" asks Cool Papa.

"Well, certainly, but..." Cool Papa takes a step toward the desk, and bends down toward Griffith. He's vexed. Something's wrong.

"Mister Griffith, last year the Senators finished 6th out of 8 teams," says Cool Papa. "Your star pitcher, Jimmie DeShong, was 14 and 15 with an ERA of 4.90. Satchel here will win you 30 games, maybe 32. Your catcher, Rick Ferrell, hit .229 with 1 home run. Josh Gibson will hit .380, with 50 home runs. Your center fielder, Mel Almada, had 12 stolen bases. You put me in center, I'll steal 80 sacks without breaking a sweat and chase down fly balls Almada couldn't catch with a butterfly net on a bicycle."

"Look..." says Griffith, but Cool Papa is just getting warmed up.

"Last year, the Senators drew 397,799 fans. That's *pathetic*. With the three of us – in fact, with Satchel Paige alone, the greatest showman in baseball, your attendance will at least *double*, maybe even *triple*. That's money in your pocket."

"Mr. Bell, with all due respect..." says Griffith, but Cool Papa's still not through.

"Respect!" shouts Cool Papa. "That's what it's all about, isn't it? What we want is some *respect*. You asked us what we're talking about here. We're talking about a straight-up tryout, just like you'd give any white player. And if we pass, as you and I both know we will, then you, Clark Griffith, will tender us contracts to play for the Washington Senators Baseball Club during the 1938 season, breaking the color line. And when that happens, you and I both know we will help your sad sack team win the World Series, and you will go down as one of the great heroes in the fight against race prejudice in America."

Whew and hallelujah! I feel like waving the flag after Cool Papa's speech. Unfortunately, the man that Cool Papa is trying to convince is sitting there flummoxed, working his jaw like there's a raspberry seed in his dentures.

"Boys," says Mr. Griffith, "I'm...I'm sorry."

"Sorry? Sorry 'bout what?" asks Josh.

"What's goin' on, Mr. Griffith?" asks Satch. Griffith unbends from behind the big desk and shuffles over to the easel.

"I want to make history. You bet I do. I want to do it by signing you three boys as the stars and part owners – yes, you will own 15% of this enterprise – of America's premiere Zulu team." And with that, he pulls the curtain off the easel, and we all see what he has in mind.

I feel like Gorilla Smith has hit me in the stomach with his best left-right combination. The other guys just stand there, staring. What we see is an advertising poster that shows cartoon versions of Josh, Satch, and Cool Papa dressed up like African "Zulus" – black fright wigs on their heads, white circles painted around their eyes, and white circles painted on their stomachs like the rings of an archery target. They're barefoot, wearing grass skirts. "Josh" holds a bat that looks like a tree trunk whittled into a war club. The poster says:

Today Only!
JOSH GIBSON!
SATCHEL PAIGE!
COOL PAPA BELL!
THE ZULU CANNIBAL CLOWNS!
Oddest Novelty in Baseball vs.
Florida Colored Hoboes
Fun! Laughs! Baseball!

The poster shows big-lipped cartoon black people laughing at the players, "Ha Ha Ha!"

"Oh...my...god," whispers Cool Papa.

"If this isn't the biggest bunch of off-time jive..." mumbles Satch. Josh stares at Griffith.

"*That's* why you brought us here?" says Josh.

"I already signed Spec Bebop – you know, the dwarf? And his buddy, King Tut," says Griffith. "They'll handle the comedy, all you boys have to do is play a little baseball."

"In a grass skirt," says Josh.

"And war paint," says Satch.

"Zulu teams are the big thing now," says Griffith. "The Ethiopian Jesters are selling out wherever they play. And you'll have a piece of the action! I thought you boys would jump at the chance."

"We AIN'T BOYS! We're MEN, dammit! MEN!" shouts Josh, rattling the windows. Deacon Powell talks about the "wrath of God." That's what's coming out of Josh right now.

"Josh, listen," says Griffith, but Josh cuts him off.

"No, just for once, *you* listen, Mr. Griffith. *You* ain't spent seven years of your life riding rickety busses down bumpy dirt roads to play three games on a single day on rocky sandlots only to get cheated out of your money, and then get turned away at the hotel for havin' the wrong paint job. *You* ain't never had to eat cold, greasy food for weeks on end, or had to catch forty winks on top of a grassy grave in a colored graveyard because every other door in town was closed." Not just Mr. Griffith, EVERYONE is staring at Josh. All that wrath is pouring out of him and it's making him sound just like the Deacon. "Sir, we came here to play baseball for the *Washington damn Senators*. You *need* us, and we need the chance to show people what we can do – not in Scofield, Alabama, or Woodville, Mississippi, or Grove Hill, Alabama, but in *Washington, D.C., Boston, Chicago, and New Damn York!*"

Silence blankets the room. Josh is sweating as he backs away from the Senators owner, his rage spent. Finally, Mr. Griffith pulls a cigar out of his inside coat pocket, bites off the tip, and spits it into a wire wastebasket. He pulls a wooden kitchen match out of the crystal holder on his desk and lights it by scratching its yellow nib with his thumbnail. Then he ignites the cigar and takes several puffs. "You boys have to face facts." At first, he was using "boy" without thinking about it. This time I know he's using it on purpose. "Washington, D.C. is a Southern city. We're still fighting the Civil War here, and the South is winning. White fans will *not* pay to see black players." Satchel snorts like a racehorse on a chilly day.

"They sure as hell pay to see us when we play – and BEAT – Mister Dizzy Dean and his so-called 'All-Star' team," says Satchel.

"That's different," barks Griffith. "That's whites on one team, your kind on the other. Hell, half of those fans want to see baseball, and the other half want to see a race war on the field. Fans won't pay to see whites and coloreds all mixed up together."

"How do you KNOW?" shouts Cool Papa. He's been standing there like a coiled watch spring. "General John J. Pershing told everybody that he didn't want black soldiers fighting for America in World War I, because they'd run away when the first shell went off. Those black soldiers got in the fight anyway. Know what the French called them? 'The Hell Fighters.' They fought, and they won every medal for valor the Army gave out, and they died – that's right, they *died* for this country, Mr. Griffith." Cool Papa Bell stops yelling, and his voice goes quiet. "Are you honestly going to tell us," he says, "that it's okay for black men to get cut in half by a German machine gun for the greater glory of America, but it's some kind of crime for them to play *a damn game of baseball?"*

"Well said, Mister Bell," says Griffith. "I'm sure everyone here is real impressed by your little oration." Pause, puff, pause. "So what happens if I sign you boys to a contract, and opening day rolls around...." Griffith pauses, takes a long pull on his cigar and puffs a perfect smoke ring into the air, "...and on opening day absolutely nobody shows up, because the entire stadium is surrounded by fellas wearing shiny white hooded robes, holding rifles and ax handles? And what happens *after* the game when you boys try to leave the stadium and the same bunch with the rifles and ax handles make it their business to grab you, drag you out to some woods right near here, and string you up?" Cool Papa starts to reply, but Griffith cuts him off. "You probably have an opinion about whether that will or won't happen, but how do you KNOW?" Griffith's words – or should I say Cool Papa's words coming back at him, out of Mr. Griffith's mouth – are like daggers. Griffith rocks back in his chair as he points to the Zulu Cannibal Clowns poster. "So there it is, boys. Playing in the big leagues – at least for the Washington Senators – is a pipe dream. No other owner is going to be this generous. Take it or leave it."

In the two weeks I've been with the team, I've seen the Crawfords get beat pretty bad, but that was just ballgames. They never took it hard. Cool Papa always says, "Shake it off, just one game, let's get 'em tomorrow." This is something else. Now my guys look plain whipped. Satch is shaking his head, and Josh is hunched over, a haunted look on his face.

Nothing left to say to Mr. Griffith. No handshakes, no polite words. We turn and head back out into the waiting room. Secretary has a sassy "I told you so" look on her face. We're almost out the door when, for no good reason I can figure, Josh stops. Then he turns back, and stares at Goose Goslin's bat. He picks it up and shoulders it like he's getting' ready to step into the batter's box. The Secretary says, "I thought I told you not to...."

It happens so fast we barely have time to be shocked. Josh rears back like he's John Henry about to use his forty-pound hammer to knock a railroad-size hole in Big Bend Mountain. The bat crashes into that glass trophy case with the four loving cups. It's like somebody set off a bomb – a crack of thunder, a billion shards of glass exploding everywhere, the clang of the metal loving cups crashing to the marble floors, the screams of the Secretary. And then all that's left is the echo of what happened and Josh, arms bloody from the glass shards, holding the bat at his side.

Then, as calm as can be, Josh places the bat back in the rack. He nods at the Secretary who is cowering under her desk, and then opens the door and walks out. Our feet crunch on the glass shards as we trail after him.

CHAPTER NINE

We stop at the Busy Bee Diner, Lord knows why. Nobody says anything and nobody eats anything but me, and I just have a strawberry milk shake. Satchel takes out Dr. Aybar's card and puts it on the counter. "Satchel's the one they want. Let Satchel do the negotiatin'."

Now we're standing at the door of Room 313 at the Hotel Washburn. Satchel knocks on the door with a "shave and a haircut, two bits" rap. Dr. Aybar opens the door and smiles. He's my idea of class. I make a mental note, so I can dress like this when I become Mr. Greenlee's right-hand man. He's dressed in a silk smoking jacket – red velvet with a shawl collar, turned-up cuffs and big brass buttons. He looks like a movie star.

As we walk in, Josh asks, "How'd you know the Senators were gonna jive us?"

"As great as your talents are, Señor Gibson," says Aybar, "the grip of race prejudice, with the ignorance and fear that reinforce it, is even greater. I have observed Mr. Griffith and his baseball club. It will take someone of great moral fortitude to place Negro players such as yourselves alongside white players. Mr. Griffith does not possess this quality. He is a merchant selling a product – nothing more, nothing less."

Now the players are lined up on the couch – Josh on one end, Cool Papa in the middle, and Satch on the other end. Dr. Aybar is parked in an easy chair. I sit cross-legged on the floor.

"So," says Satch, "Just so's we know what we're getting' ourselves into, give it to us one more time. The whole kit and caboodle."

"Especially the caboodle," says Cool Papa. Aybar smiles that small, sly smile.

"Just so," he says. "You, Señor Paige, and eight of your hand-picked compatriots will be flown at Dr. Trujillo's expense to the Dominican Republic."

"First class," says Satchel. It's not a question.

"First class, of course. On the Pan American Clipper. You will be greeted by the Dominican people as the baseball deities you are. My country is entirely free of the appalling race prejudice of the United States. There you will play in a five game baseball exhibition, with games every other day. You will win three of these five games, at which time you will be free to stay in our country for however long you wish, or return to the United States and your current team, the Pittsburgh Crawfords."

"Win three outta five," says Cool Papa, pondering.

"Naturally, the Great Benefactor will be delighted if you win the first three games, eliminating the need to play all five," says Aybar.

"What if we don't win?" asks Josh. Aybar seems surprised by this question, as if this hasn't occurred to him.

"Ah, but you will. You are the best in the world," says Aybar. Josh opens his mouth but Satch jumps in.

"Damn straight. With Satchel on the mound, we can beat anybody. Anytime, anywhere. 'Specially a bunch of local boys."

"Short series, Satch," says Cool Papa, brow furrowed. "Anything can happen." He turns to Aybar. "If we don't win…will we have to give the money back?" Aybar laughs at this.

"No, my friend. The money is yours no matter what. However…" Aybar pauses, trying to find words, "there is one complicating factor you might wish to know about." Everyone's ears prick up at this nugget.

"Complicating factor?" says Cool Papa.

"What is it?" asks Josh.

"A great election will be held the day after the final game, if the series goes to five games. The Dominican people will be asked to ratify the inspired and enterprising leadership of our Beloved and Universally Revered Sovereign, Rafael Trujillo."

"What do these…how does this…" Cool Papa struggles for the right question. Josh jumps in.

"He's bringin' us in to make him look good before the people vote. That about it?" For the first time since I laid eyes on him, Aybar looks nervous. He brushes the front of his smoking jacket, and then returns Josh's gaze.

"Opponents of our Exalted Benefactor – interests from outside our country, brought in to cause unrest and dissatisfaction – have made it their business to tell lies and spread fear." Now Aybar's gaze sweeps the whole room. He is dead serious, and talks like he's sharing a secret. "El Jefe feels the need to show his beneficence. Our people love baseball with a passion that exceeds reason."

"I'm startin' to understand that," says Josh.

"I have traveled your United States these last months, at his behest, to find the very best players. I have seen games in every city in America. I have seen the great DiMaggio play, as well as Lou Gehrig, Joe Medwick, Lefty Gomez and Carl Hubbell. As good as they are, they are merely great – not the greatest. *You* are the greatest players in the world. *You* are the ones who will show the Dominican people that they are destined to achieve greatness, under the guidance of Dr. Trujillo."

"The greatest players in the world make the most money. Stands to reason." Satchel has raised the stakes in this card game.

"I am authorized to offer..." begins Aybar, but Satch cuts him off.

"Ol' Satch ain't interested in what you're 'authorized' to offer, Doc. Let Satch tell you what it's gonna cost you. Nine players, two weeks more or less, victory guaranteed...that's gonna cost you twenty...thousand...dollars." Cool Papa lets out a low whistle. That's a year's worth of barnstorming, and then some. Pretty bold move. Aybar looks surprised.

"Oh," says Aybar, rubbing his chin. "Most unfortunate." Satch lets out a loud sigh, and looks at the guys with a weary "I knew it" smirk as Dr. Aybar grabs a suitcase made of brown cowhide leather and plops it on his lap. He springs the two latches and opens it up. Inside is more cash money than I've ever seen in my life, and I've been inside the policy bank of Mister Benny Melrose when he was loading a day's take into his steel cashbox for a trip to the bank. I'm staring at a suitcase full of cash money, in banded bricks of ten-dollar bills. "I was authorized to offer you *thirty* thousand dollars. However, if twenty will suffice..."

"Thirty'll do just fine," says Satch, a little too loudly.

"That's a lot of money," says Josh nervously.

"Couple o' year's worth," says Cool Papa.

"That's because...as I'm certain you've guessed by now...I have *guaranteed* El Presidente that he is paying not just for your presence, but for a victory in the upcoming series. Will that be a problem? Because if it is, you must tell me now, so we can negotiate an adjustment in the price."

Satch bends over, bumps the top of the suitcase closed, flips it around and snaps the latches. He curls his big hand around the handle, and pauses. Dr. Aybar nods, and Satch pulls the suitcase off Aybar's lap.

"No need to re-negotiate nothin', Doc. You tell Mister 'El Big Shot Presidente Trujillo Grande' that Satchel Paige done *guaranteed* him a victory." Satch turns and looks at Josh. "Straight-up sure thing." He turns back to Aybar. "He can take that promise to the bank and cash a check against it. The only question is how many games it's going to take us, which translates to how often Satchel feels like exerting himself on the big stage."

And that's how the deal goes down. Everybody shakes everybody else's hand. Aybar pours some drinks. Everybody knocks 'em back and shouts "Victory!" And all I have to do is figure out what to tell Mister Gus Greenlee, and how to convince Mama to let me go.

CHAPTER TEN

"Josh?"

"Yeah, Peanut?" I've worked a switch with Deacon Powell so's I can park myself next to Josh on the Crawfords bus heading back to Pittsburgh. I need a friend.

"I, ummm…that is, I have a confession to make."

"Uh huh."

"You fellas like the job I'm doing? As batboy?"

Josh laughed. "Best we ever had, Peanut. That's why we're takin' you with us. You're our good luck charm."

"Well, ummm…maybe not. See, the whole reason I got this job was so that…so that…."

"So that you could snitch us out to Gus Greenlee. He told you to spy on us, right? 'Specially Satch, if I'm not mistaken."

My mouth drops open. Huh? "You knew? How'd you know that?"

Josh horse-laughs. "He does that with *every* batboy, Peanut. He's a snake. Don't fret about it."

Now I'm confused. "You mean...I shouldn't...I mean, I feel duty bound to let him know...."

Josh turns toward me, squares himself and stares me right in the eye, serious for the first time. "Peanut, you remember what happened to Cornell Taft after he busted his leg slidin' into second against the Eagles up there in Newark?"

"Yeah. The team left him behind."

Josh leans so close to my face I can feel the heat of his breath. "No, Peanut. *The team* didn't leave him behind. *Gus Greenlee* left him behind. He ordered us to ditch him, toss him out like garbage. And we know he'd ditch any of us if we got busted up. I owe the guys on this team, Peanut. They got my back. I don't owe Greenlee a damn thing, and neither do you."

I flashed on that moment in the clearing, Josh stepping in front of three shotguns and a noose for me. Man, did he have my back then. Couldn't see Gus doing that, unless I had a chunk of change belonged to him. Maybe there was something in life bigger than a dollar bill. "Yeah. I see your point. Thanks, Josh." He turned to face forward, slumped in his seat, pulled his cap over his eyes, and went to sleep.

October 10, 1937

CRAWFORDS COURIER SPECIAL "ADIOS" EDITION

"CREAM OF THE CRAWFORDS" TAPPED FOR DOMINICAN BASEBALL TOURNEY

EXCLUSIVE to Clyde "Peanut" Wiggins – Editor and Senior Writer, Crawfords Courier

"We're taking a two week baseball vacation in paradise," Crawfords pitching ace Satchel Paige told this reporter on Sunday. "The President of the Dominican Republic, Rafael Trujillo, has asked Satchel Paige to put together a team of the greatest players in the Negro Leagues to represent his country. How could Satchel refuse this great honor?"

Paige named the eight players who will go with him for this exciting five game international tournament:

COOL PAPA BELL – fleet 34-year-old center fielder, who will also serve as team manager. Bell currently leads the Negro National League with 44 stolen sacks.

JOSH GIBSON – "The Sepia Sultan of Swat" tops the league in round-trippers (23), runs batted in (67), and has the third best batting average (.361).

PAYDAY THOMPSON – This rangy (6'4") first-sacker is second in homers for the Crawfords, with 11. He has found a home in Pittsburgh after playing for five other teams in the Negro National League.

LUTHER "DEACON" POWELL – The 37-year-old veteran shortstop will be an invaluable "special coach" for Manager Bell. The Deacon speaks fluent Spanish, having played 11 seasons of winter ball in Venezuela, Cuba, and Mexico. (And yes, he is an actual "New Testament Deacon" in the Baptist Church!)

LITTLE WILLIE TATUM – The Crawfords 17-year-old rookie second-sack sensation has 56 doubles, 11 triples and 19 stolen bases. He has teamed with Powell for 89 twin killings, best in the NNL.

"BULLET" HAMPTON – "Got to have my man Bullet with us," Satchel Paige told this reporter about the 33-year-old right fielder Hampton. "Man can pitch when I get tuckered out, play outfield, pinch hit and rub down my arm with that special snake oil of his."

"FLASH" FOWLER – Fowler is the Crawfords' 29-year-old keystone sack phenom, often called "the dirtiest player in the Negro Leagues" because his uniform gets so filthy from his hell-for-leather base running antics.

BOOKER SAMUELS – Left-fielder Samuels has the lowest average of the Crawfords' starting nine (.246), but makes up for it with his speed, his heads-up play, his fielding prowess and his expertise at the hit-and-run.

Your faithful scribe, "Peanut" Wiggins, will accompany the players to the Dominican, and will post a full report of the tournament on his return.

Cool Papa Bell – a genius in addition to being the ace center fielder in baseball and a swell guy besides – figured out the perfect way to handle Mama when we all got together in our kitchen over pecan pie and coffee. "You happy with the way things are goin'?" he asked her.

"Well, I s'pose. Peanut seems to be working hard..."

"Didn't you read my letter, Mama?" I say. "I'm working my butt...er, that is, I'm very busy all the time."

"Yes. And he is writing to me just as I asked."

"And," added Josh, "He hasn't been jumped by hooligans like when he was running numbers."

"True," said Mama.

"There's been a new wrinkle in the saga, Lila. We have an exciting new opportunity."

"Mmmmm," she said, pouring Cool Papa some more coffee. She was looking skeptical, like he was a door-to-door brush salesman and she didn't want no brushes. Here's where the genius part came in. Rather than tell her where we were going, he pulled a check out of his pocket.

"This is for you...or rather, for Peanut." She looked it over, and her eyes went real wide. She plunked down in her chair, holding the check with both hands, staring at it.

"A...a thousand dollars?"

"Made out to your name as administrator of the Clyde 'Peanut' Wiggins Higher Education Fund." A thousand bucks is what the other eight guys decided to give me after Satchel took half the $30,000.

"So...what is this 'opportunity'?" Instead of skeptical, she had hope in her eyes, and a little fear. My heart raced. I knew we had her, if...

"A select group of Crawfords players has been asked by El Presidente Rafael Trujillo to represent his country, the Dominican Republic, in an elite one-week baseball tournament."

"You want Peanut to...to go with you? You want to take him out of the country?"

Cool Papa smiled. "Lila, this is a once-in-a-lifetime chance to visit a friend of the United States on a goodwill tour, sponsored by the government with first-class air fare and deluxe accommodations."

She looked at him, then at me, and then at the check. She put the check in her lap.

"Mama," I said, but before I could finish, Josh stepped in.

"I'll still look after him, Lila. No matter what happens, he'll be safe. Got my word." Then Mama grabbed me into a ferocious hug and started to cry, and I looked over her shoulder at Cool Papa smiling at me. I smiled right back.

That all happened yesterday. Now all we have to do is get out of the country.

The plan is to take the Quaker City Zephyr to Richmond, Virginia, then transfer to the Sunshine State Flyer down to Miami, where we'll catch the Pam Am Clipper to the Dominican Republic. Good plan – until we walk up to the ticket counter at Penn Station. There, blocking our way, is six feet, two inches and 240 pounds of gun-wielding bluster. I have no idea how Mister Gus Greenlee found us out – I sure didn't tell him – but there he is, backed up by his lawyer, Gorilla Smith, Bonecrusher Doaks, a white policeman, and a reporter from the *Pittsburgh Courier*. Gus looks daggers at me, then walks right up to Dr. Aybar and pokes him in the chest with the pistol. "Lookie here, you – you kidnapper! These are MY boys! I got 'em under CONTRACT!"

"Contract?" asks Josh, puzzled. "We don't even have a handshake."

"Well, I got HIM under contract," says Greenlee, pointing to Satchel.

"He tells me he wishes to play for the Dominican people," says Dr. Aybar.

"That's gospel, Brother Aybar," says Satch. Gus Greenlee is in the business of getting his way, which is the opposite of what's happening here. He turns and bellows at Dr. Aybar.

"Why don't you raid the white leagues if you need a team?" The louder Greenlee gets, the more relaxed Aybar becomes.

"Because," he says calmly, "our Noble Benefactor told me to bring back the *best*." Satch perks up when he hears this.

"Yeah," says Satch, "and we're gettin' paid what we're *worth*, not that chump change you dole out."

"Satch," says Greenlee, "If you get on that train...if you leave the country...if you jump the Crawfords, you're banned from the Negro National League *for life!* Think about it!" Satch smiles.

"Hmmmm. Didn't you ban ol' Satch once before, Gus? 'Bout two years ago? Banned him for life that time too, as I recall it. And then when folks stopped comin' to your fine ball field you hired ol' Satchel right back, with a big damn raise, and he won you the damn pennant." All true. Satchel has Greenlee, and Gus knows it. Gus looks at Josh and Cool Papa, then back at Satch. Then he turns to the policeman.

"Arrest these men!" he barks.

"Okay. Uhhhhhh... What have they done?" asks the cop. Greenlee turns to the lawyer.

"Tell him what they've done."

"Well," says the lawyer, "Technically, since they haven't left yet, they haven't actually done anything."

"But they're about to do something!" splutters Greenlee.

"I can't arrest them for what they're about to do," says the cop.

"Fact is," says Satchel, "ol' Satch can't hear a word you're saying, Gus. Now, 'Long Daddy Green,' Satch can hear that cat loud and clear." Satch is holding the brown leather suitcase. He jerks it up and cradles it in one arm as he flips the latches, opens it with the other, and pushes it in Gus's face. Gus looks like he's suddenly staring down the barrel of a loaded gun.

"But...but..." stammers Greenlee.

"Long Daddy Green is sayin', 'Adios, amigo." Satch slams down the lid of the suitcase and walks right past him to the ticket counter as the rest of us follow, leaving Gus and his bunch standing there open-mouthed and flat-footed.

CHAPTER ELEVEN

October 11, 1937

I am closer to heaven than I've ever been, or ever expect to be again. I am flying over the Atlantic on the Pan Am Clipper, the "Ocean Liner of the Air." I am sitting in a cushy leather seat, with a porthole next to me so can I watch the fluffy white clouds float by. I am eating a steak and baked potato dinner, which is just about the best thing I've ever tasted, including my grandma's smothered pork chops. I'm listening to the sweet music of Satch, Josh, Cool Papa, and the rest of the fellows laughin' and cuttin' up because they are so happy to be off that rickety bus, on their way to a big paycheck, being treated like they've always wanted to be treated.

Dr. Aybar is sitting next to Satchel, who has not stopped talking since we took off, about five hours ago. Satchel has an opinion about everything. Right now he's telling Dr. Aybar that the Exalted Protector of the Dominican Citizenry might consider paying Satchel an additional ten thousand dollars to introduce him at campaign rallies, since Satchel is going to be so popular after he shows the Dominican people what real American baseball is, and what the best player in the world can do in person.

Josh also has a window seat, next to Cool Papa. Payday Thompson is next to Deacon Powell, who is on his second steak dinner. Amazing what a skinny guy like him can put away. Booker Powell is next to Maximo Borgatti, which doesn't seem to make either one very happy. I'm sitting next to big, friendly white man in a gaudy Hawaiian shirt, cream-colored pants, black and white spectator shoes and a brand new Panama hat. His name is Tyler Underwood, and he must be some kind of baseball fan, because he keeps asking questions about our guys. "This is just about the whole Crawfords squad, isn't it?"

"Just about," I say.

"Weren't you boys just on the road? Down in Georgia or something?"

"Alabama," I say. "How you know that?"

"They must be tired," he says as he sips his martini. I know it's a martini because it's in that special cone-shaped glass and it has a green olive in it. Mister Wonderful Jones, bartender at the Crawford Club, Mr. Gus Greenlee's private third floor party room, showed me how to make one. He showed me how to make all the most popular alcohol drinks when my mom wasn't around. I can even make a "Zombie," which has two kinds of rum and apricot brandy.

"Josh, Satchel, Cool Papa – they NEVER get tired of playin' baseball," I say. "Tired of them rickety busses, yes. Tired of bed bugs and bad food, you bet. But playin' ball? They'll do that at the drop of a hat, and they'll drop their own hats. So why are *you* on this plane? Are you comin' over for the games?" I ask him.

"They ever play ball in the Dominican?" he asks. Guy asks a lot of questions without ever answering any of mine.

"Not that I know. Couple of the boys play winter ball in Cuba. What's it like, where we're goin'?"

"How come you're not in school?" he asks.

"Why you want to know that?"

"Just curious," he says.

"You a cop? Or a teacher?"

"How'd Gus Greenlee feel about his boys jumping the league?"

"How come I answer all your questions and you dodge all mine?" I answer. He chuckles and nods…but dodges my question again.

"'Scuse me, son," he says, hoisting his big frame out of his seat. As he makes for Satchel, I spoon a mouthful of the melty vanilla ice cream off his tray. "Satchel!" booms Mister Underwood. "You are the great Satchel Paige, aren't you?" I got a great seat to watch all this.

"That's right," says Satch. "And you are…"

"This is Señor Tyler Underwood," says Dr. Aybar, surprising Satch.

"Doctor Aybar, how you doing?" says Underwood. "Looks like your little shopping trip paid off. You got everything you wanted."

"Yes, I'm sure the Great Benefactor will be very happy, knowing that the very best…" but before he can finish, Underwood swivels back to Satchel, who has his face down in his steak dinner.

"I saw you strike out that DiMaggio kid last year. My god, you were throwing aspirin tablets! Never seen anybody throw a baseball like that. You're terrific!" Satchel is bit taken aback by this burst of enthusiasm from a white man, but he quickly recovers.

"Satchel is the best there is. Unbeaten and unbeatable. You got one game to win it all, ol' Satch is who you want on the mound," says Satch, just stating the natural fact as he continues to eat.

"And how are your Sugar Kings, Mister Underwood?" says Dr. Aybar. Now things click into place. This guy's a big shot with the other team!

"Well, first of all," he says, "they're not 'my' Sugar Kings, Doctor. They belong to the people of San Pedro de Macoris. The Combine just provides a little…you know…financial support." By now several of the Crawfords are privy to this confab. Dr. Aybar lays it out for Satch, Josh, and Cool Papa.

"Señor Underwood is an influential part of the 'Combine' – a group of American sugar companies with plantations in our country." Aybar is smiling, but it ain't a friendly smile. Kind of like a cobra smiles at a frog as he's getting' ready to gobble it up. Underwood stays fixed on Satch the whole time.

"I've got a question for you, Mr. Paige," he says.

"The answer is no," says Satch.

"No?"

"No, the Sugar Kings ain't got a chance. No way, no how. They are dead and buried. Just don't know it yet."

Underwood laughs. "Oh, I know that already." This gets Satchel's attention. He finally looks up from his steak.

"You do?"

"'Course."

"So then," says Satch, "what's your question?" Underwood leans down, which naturally makes everyone else lean in toward him. I move up next to Cool Papa, so I can hear better.

"After this series is over...I mean, after you whip us...would you lads be interested in making some *real* money?" As Underwood says this, I can see Satchel's eyes widen just a bit.

"Depends what you call real money," says Satch. "Seeing as how Satchel Paige is currently the best paid ballplayer in the world."

Underwood leans in even closer, so close he's practically whispering. "How much is Dr. Aybar here paying you to pitch in this series?" Satch looks both ways, like he's about to reveal a military secret.

"Fifty thousand," lies Satch. Underwood steals a quick glance at Dr. Aybar, who stays poker-faced.

"And that's split, what, nine ways?" asks Underwood.

"Satch takes what he wants, doles out the rest eight ways, as he sees fit."

"What if I told you," says Underwood, pausing so's everyone is hangin' on his every word, "that people I know could put together more money than any baseball player has ever been paid anywhere in the world..."

"Yeah?" asks Satch. He's like a fish lookin' at a big, fat, juicy worm without seein' the hook.

"...and we'd pay you, Satchel Paige, this money to head up the 'Satchel Paige International Goodwill All-Stars.' We'd set up exhibitions all over the globe, playing the best of the best."

"Best of the best..." Satch parrots his words, testing them out.

"You betcha. We'll really put the 'world' into the "World Series."

"Nice uniforms?" says Satch, startin' to look dreamy.

"You design 'em yourself."

"No busses," says Satch.

"Trains only, first-class all the way."

"No ratty sandlots."

"Big league ballparks and stadiums only."

"We stay in real hotels? No boarding houses, or campin' out?" he asks warily.

"You, my friend, would have your own Pullman train car, a luxury hotel on wheels, with a porter at your beck and call to serve you just the food you want – meals like this one here – whenever you want it."

"Mister Underwood," says Satchel, "You and Satchel Paige might be able to do some business. SERIOUS business. As soon as the fellas wrap up whatever we got goin' on here in the Dominican, let's us have a chin wag."

"I would be delighted. You're like a great actor, Mr. Paige. It's about time somebody built you a stage worthy of your talents." And with that, Underwood shakes Satch's hand, then turns and sits next to Josh, since Deacon Powell has moved into the seat next to mine.

"What do you make of that, Deacon?"

"Do you know what Jesus promised his followers, young master Clyde?"

"No, I surely don't."

"He promised three things. They would be absurdly happy, entirely fearless, and always in trouble. Let us bask in the revealed wisdom of our risen and living spiritual exemplar." With that, he shuts his eyes and falls right into a sound sleep.

The Stewardess comes through and tells us we're going to be landing in 'bout an hour. Seems like a great big adventure we got ahead of us, but I can't shake the feelin' that somethin' about it ain't right.

CHAPTER TWELVE

The plane skids, skitters and bumps as it hits the water, and I can feel all that steak and baked potato bump along with it. Finally the plane turns into a boat and we float up to the dock. That's when the real surprises start. Before we can get off the plane, the hatch opens and a whirlwind flies in. "Welcome, American gods of baseball! My name is Julissa Perez, personal assistant to the Great Benefactor of the Dominican Nation, Rafael Leonidas Trujillo Molina." She's a tall, slender, movie-star-pretty stick of dynamite dressed in tailored khaki army fatigues. Her black hair is tucked inside a baseball cap with a dragon on it. "A very special welcome has been prepared for you, and I will have the honor of capturing this glorious moment on film. What I want – the reason I'm here – is to give you permission to be what you are."

"What we are?" says Josh. "We're baseball players."

"Gettin' paid," says Satchel, "to do a job."

"No, Señor Paige," says Julissa. "Señor Gibson, Señor Satchel Paige, Señor Cool Papa Bell, ALL of you – you are not baseball players. You are gods. GODS! Ascending from the heavens to assist us here in the Dominican Republic so that we can achieve our destiny – a destiny that can be described in a single word – VICTORY!" The fellas practically fall over backwards when she hollers this last word. She is on fire! She looks straight at Josh as she says, "Stand tall. Embrace your destiny. Let my cameras see the fierce pride that radiates from your confidence that you will achieve this victory. Drink in the adulation that is about to be heaped upon you. Gentlemen, this is your moment. Savor it." Then she smiles, nods, turns and hops off the plane. The fellas look at each other. What's going on?

The second I poke my head out of the plane I can see the newsreel cameras, along with a bunch of soldiers and fans – LOTS of fans. This crowd is big enough for a Sunday afternoon double-header at Greenlee Field. They're holding signs that say "BIENVENIDOS DRAGONES DE TRUJILLO" and cheering their heads off as we step off the plane. "Los Fanaticos Locos," says Underwood, who is gettin' off the plane just behind me.

"What?" I say.

"Dominican fans. They're somethin' else – the craziest fans you've ever seen. You think Crawfords fans are wild? You ain't seen nothin' yet, my young friend. The newspaper calls them 'Los Fanaticos Locos.' They live and die with the Dominican team."

The second surprise happens when I take my first deep breath. The air! Wow! As a resident of Pittsburgh, PA, I'm used to breathing pretty nasty stuff – sharp, sooty, murky, with a little burn for your lungs. It's the air that's belched out of the smokestacks of all those steel plants. The air here is…is…what is it like? Well, you can't see it, for one thing. I look up – the sky is blue, not smoke-gray. And it's got some water in it. Humid, like down in Alabama and Georgia. Balmy. And then there's the smell – sweet, gentle, like the air inside Hazel Tucker's Florist Shop when the fresh orchids come in. Feels good inside my body. I WANT to breathe this stuff!

The third surprise – and I don't even know why this should surprise me, but it does – is somethin' all the fellas feel, because I can see it in their faces as they walk off the plane. Everybody here – the players, the fans, the soldiers, the porters – has the same dusky paint job, just different shades. Me and Satch and Josh and Cool Papa are a little blacker, and "Los Fanaticos Locos" are little more coffee-colored, but its like…I dunno…we're all on the same side. I feel like I can relax a little, for the first time in my life. I feel something let go in my chest, a kind of nervous fear. Feels *good* to be here.

About the soldiers. No police here, just soldiers with shiny chrome helmets, fancy uniforms and big rifles with bayonets. Not friendly whatsoever, but not lookin' at us like they can't wait to put us in the jug. I'll settle for that.

"You're gods! GODS!" screams Julissa as Payday Thompson starts to walk down the gangplank. He puffs his chest out, throws his shoulders back, and does his best to look god-like. He gets a huge cheer, waves at the newsreel camera, and then gets jumped by a bunch of fans. He starts to fight back until he figures out what they're up to – they're hoisting him on their shoulders so they can carry him to the fire-engine red De Soto convertible car that's going to carry him to the big welcome rally.

One by one each player acts god-like walking the gangplank, gets a huge cheer, waves at the cameras, gets hoisted up by the fans, and gets plopped into his own convertible. Josh is the next to last down the gangplank. No acting here – he's naturally god-like. It takes nine guys to carry him to the De Soto, and when he gets plonked down in the back seat he's sitting next to Julissa Perez. She waits for the newsreel cameras to catch her, then hands a bunch of flowers to Josh, smiles and waves. I sneak into the front seat of their car, next to the driver.

The final Crawford down the gangplank is, of course, Satchel Paige. He takes Julissa's direction to heart – he steps out of the plane, raises his arms to acknowledge the thundering screams of love, then struts down the gangplank like an African prince on his way to the coronation. He gets just what he wants

– the biggest cheer, the biggest bunch of fans to carry him to his car, and the biggest car. It's a mammoth red and black Rolls-Royce Phantom III Touring Limousine, like the one that Gus Greenlee sits in during the Pittsburgh Labor Day Parade. And when he gets lowered down in the back seat, Satch gets the best looking woman. "That's Nova Quezada," says Julissa. "She is El Presidente Trujillo's favorite movie actress. They have a very special relationship." All five newsreel cameras move in to capture this on film.

I'm still breathin' that sweet, clean jasmine air as we cruise toward the big welcome rally that Dr. Trujillo is throwin' for us. Josh is preoccupied talkin' to Julissa, so he doesn't see what I see. And what I see is the *amount* of Trujillo they've got here in Ciudad Trujillo. I mean, I work for Gus Greenlee, who thinks that he's the original Mister Big Stuff, but he's got *nothin'* on this Trujillo fella.

Every street corner, intersection and vacant lot has a giant Trujillo statue. We pass "Plaza Trujillo," "Parque Trujillo," "Calle Trujillo," "Avenida Trujillo," and "Jardines de Trujillo." I see five billboards that show off the steely truant officer face of Dr. Trujillo next to the slogan, "Exaltado Benefactor de la Patria." And every church I see has a banner that reads, "Dios En El Cielo, Trujillo En La Tierra." "What's that mean?" I ask the driver.

Without looking at me, he mutters, "God In The Sky, Trujillo On The Earth."

Creepy.

We drive up to some huge golden gates and I start to hear something – like the low rumble of an incoming thunderstorm. The closer we get, the louder it gets. Then we roll through those gates onto the grounds of the Presidential Palace and we find ourselves in the middle of what must be a hundred thousand people, all screaming their heads off. The only thing that keeps them from mobbing us is the double line of soldiers using the bayonets on their rifles to hold them back.

Julissa Perez jumps out of our car and vaults up a ladder to the top of a 50-foot scaffold that supports three of her newsreel cameras. I look around – there must be fifteen cameras here, catching every bit of this crazy pageant. A one-hundred-piece marching band bursts into song as our limo rocks to a stop. The land yacht is in a line next to the elevated welcome stand, filled with politicians and military officers gathered around a flag-drapped podium. Behind the podium is a hundred-foot-high picture of Trujillo's face, with the words "EXALTADO BENEFACTOR" underneath. Every fan has a Dominican flag in one hand, and a Ciudad Trujillo Dragones pennant in the other.

I turn back and see Josh, drinking this all in. His eyes are wide, happiness spiked with amazement. All this whoop-de-do is for the Crawfords. Couple of days ago some crazies in bed sheets were trying to lynch Josh for the crime of being a proud black man. Now he's a god being welcomed into paradise. I stand next to Deacon Powell, 'cuz he knows Spanish, since he's played winter ball in either Cuba or Venezuela for the last ten years.

Dr. Aybar mounts the podium and steps up to the microphone. He holds out his hands to hush the crowd. "Mis Ciudadanos," he begins, "cuando se escriba la historia de nuestro gran país, ¡ESTE será uno de nuestros días mas grandes! Un día de ¡DESTINO!"

"What did he say?" I ask the Deacon.

"Says that today is a day of destiny." The crowd erupts in a huge bellow of joy. Aybar quiets them. ""Es mi gran honor presentar les su querido Presidente, Gran Benefactor de la Nación, Exaltado Protector de la ciudadanía Dominicana, Padre del Nuevo Dominio, e Ilustrado Guía de Nuestro Destino Nacional, El Presidente, Doctor Rafael Leonidas Trujillo Molina!"

"Wow," says the Deacon. "Apparently this Trujillo guy isn't just the President. He's the Great Benefactor, Exalted Protector, Father of the New Dominion, Enlightened Steward, and Grand-High Poobah of this bit of paradise."

"What's a Poobah?"

"Kiddin' about that, Peanut."

Dr. Aybar steps aside and there's Trujillo. The crowd explodes into the loudest, longest scream of ecstasy yet – must last at least two minutes. All fifteen newsreel cameras are on Trujillo as he turns his body, arms up, drinking in this adulation. When the cheering slows down a bit, two dozen soldiers shoulder their rifles and fire a welcome salute in the air, starting the whole thing all over again.

The Most Exalted Benefactor is a little shorter than I thought he'd be, and he's kind of squat – if he were a ballplayer, he'd definitely be a catcher. He's got a big round head like Gus Greenlee, but with a face the shade of café au lait, with a little Charlie Chaplin moustache under his nose. He's dressed in a red and black military get-up that's more of a costume, with a gold sash across his chest, a bunch of bronze medals hanging around his neck, and a golden scabbard at his side holding a sword. The crowd finally settles down. "Give it to me as he says it," I say to the Deacon.

"Gotcha," he says.

"Mis queridos niños," says Trujillo, "saben que todo que hago, es por el bien de ustedes."

"My beloved children, whatever I do, I do for you," says the Deacon over the cheers.

"Es por ustedes que he creado la agregación de proeza atlética mas poderosa en la historia del béisbol, incluyendo el Demonio Sepia de la velocidad, James Thomas "Cool Papa Bell!"

As Cool Papa bounds up on the podium, Deacon says, "He says that it's for these folks right here he's created the greatest team of all time, including the Sepia Speed Demon, our friend Señor Bell." Trujillo sticks out his hand, but Cool Papa grabs him in a hug.

Not sure El Presidente is ready for that, but he manages a smile as he pulls out of the clench.

"Los Dragones también contarán con el jonronero mas grande de todo el béisbol, mas poderoso que el propio Babe Ruth – el temible destructor de bardas, ¡Joshua Gibson!" Josh leaps out of the back seat and strides up to the podium.

"Catch that?" asks the Deacon.

"The greatest or biggest 'something' in all of baseball..."

"Mightiest slugger, better than Babe Ruth," smiles the Deacon. El President opens his arms for another hug, but Josh crosses him up and sticks out his hand. They shake.

"Y finalmente," says Trujillo, a big smile on his face, "Quiero que conozcan a su nuevo Capitan de los Dragones de Ciudad Trujillo." Satch strides up right next to Trujillo as the accolades continue. "El enviado por el mismísimo Dios para guiar nuestro querido equipo nacional a la victoria!"

"Says that God himself sent Satch here," shouts the Deacon over the screaming crowd.

"El inbatiable, diestro lanza fuegos conocido mundialmente. El único,....."

"Unhittable, fireballing right-hander known around the world. The one and only..." Tired of waiting, Satch cuts off Dr. Trujillo and leans into the microphone.

"Why don't you just tell 'em the truth?" says Satch. "You've wrangled the *best damn player in the history of baseball.*"

Trujillo barks a horse-laugh and says, "El mejor maldito beisbolista en la historia del béisbol, Señor Satchel Paige!!!" The screams of the crowd turn into a chant. "Sa-chel!" "Sa-chel!" "Sa-chel!" Trujillo puts one arm around Satchel, and the other around Josh. Julissa crosses in front of the podium and captures this with a hand-held "Eyemo" camera. A couple of reporters move in behind her. One yells a question. "¡Señor Presidente! Estamos a diez días de la elección?"

"Así es," says Trujillo, still drinking in the adulation of the crowd.

"¿Como serán afectado sus posibilidades, si el equipo Dominicano llegará a perder la serie?" I look at the Deacon.

"Election in ten days. Guy wants to know what happens to the Exalted Benefactor if his All-Star team gets licked."

Trujillo breaks away from the fellas and gets nose-to-nose with the reporter. "El Equipo Dominicano NO SERA DERROTADO. ¡¡El Presidente NO PIERDE!!" More cheering, more flag waving, more screams of joy. The Deacon looks at me.

"What do you think he said, Peanut?"

"We're not going to lose?"

The Deacon smiles at me. "He said the Dominican national team will not lose, and that he, El Presidente,

DOES not lose." More cheering, more flag waving, more screams of joy.

"Los Dragones son INVENCIBLES" says Trujillo. "Serán cargados sobre nubes de gloría por Díos hasta la victoria..."

"We're invincible," says the Deacon. "Carried on clouds of glory by God his bad self to victory."

Trujillo pivots and points to the colossal portrait of himself. "... ¡así como yo mismo seré cargado por el pueblo ¡Dominicano a la victoria! ¡Victoria! ¡Victoria! "

The crowd picks up the chant. "¡Victoria!" "¡Victoria!" "¡Victoria!" Trujillo smiles, and clasps his hands over his head, like a prizefighter after a knockout.

"So what do you think, young master Clyde?" The Deacon looks at me for the first time since El Presidente wound himself up.

"I think...ummm...the people around here really like baseball. And El Presidente Trujillo," I say.

"Is that so?"

"Yeah, I guess. Don't you?"

The Deacon ponders this. "Well," he says, "If you were a politician...and you had a big election coming up...and you really thought you were going to win, would you need to stage all this whangdangdoodle?" I think about this as the soldiers herd us back into the limousines. Can't spoof the Deacon. Something's up, big time.

CHAPTER THIRTEEN

Trujillo's home, the "presidential residence," is a palace – bigger than St. Luke's Church, the Carnegie Library, and the Hunt Armory put together. If Trujillo really does know God, I'm sure this is where the two of them get together and talk about running the world on Sunday morning. The ceiling is so high I can practically see angels flying around above me.

All the generals and politicians from the welcome ceremony are here, shaking hands with the fellas, asking them questions and getting their pictures taken. Satch stands at the center of the biggest group of the biggest big shots, telling jokes, signing autographs and smiling. A string quartet plays what my father used to call "long-hair music." Guys in fancy cutaway tuxedos carry trays of "pastelitos," which are like tiny meat pies only with raisins and olives. There are food tables against every wall. I walk up to one, grab a plate and say, "What you got?"

"How would you like to eat our national flag?" he says, and then he heaps my plate with the colors of the Dominican flag – white rice, red beans, and fried green plantains, which are like chewier, saltier bananas. He also spoons me up some boiled shrimp and stewed chicken. I notice little Willie Tatum watching me. He's only three years older than I am, and only four inches taller. I take a bite and give him a thumbs up, so he gets in line to get his own.

A guy behind a bar is mixing drinks – all the ones that Wonderful Jones showed me, plus something he calls a "mojito," which I gather is like the national drink here in the Dominican. Start with rum, then mix in sugar cane juice, lime, sparkling water, and a sprig of mint. I reach out for one when I feel that steel lobster claw paralyze my shoulder. It's Josh. "Think you made a mistake there, Peanut," he says, taking the drink from my hand and putting it back on the white tablecloth. Then he turns to the bartender and says, "Make him one without the firewater." At least I got a taste.

"What do you think of all this?" I ask him.

"Not bad," he says.

"Not bad?" I yelp. I can't believe he's not jumping up and down with excitement. "Josh, they're treating you like a champ! Like the way they ought to treat you back in Pittsburgh!"

"This doesn't have a single thing to do with playing baseball," he says, looking over the room. "Trujillo is showing us off for his friends, like zoo animals, to prove what a big shot he is. Let's us win a ballgame, then maybe he'll throw us a *real* party. Something that means something."

Just then we hear the string quartet play a fanfare. Dr. Aybar stands next to Trujillo and shushes the crowd. "Thank you all for joining us on this most auspicious occasion," he says. "I have excellent news. I have just learned that the American baseball players, to express their love for the Dominican people, have graciously offered to donate 10% of the moneys they will receive for representing our country to the election campaign of our Great Benefactor." Trujillo steps forward to say something, but before he can begin, a fracas breaks out. Satchel is going wild. He's stiff-arming Deacon Powell so he can get at our host.

"Uh oh," says Josh, who bolts over and tackles Satch before Satch can get at Trujillo. Everyone watches this in horror, then backs away nervously. They want no part of whatever happens next.

"Please, please! Gentlemen, in here," says Dr. Aybar, shooing everyone through a twenty-foot-high gilded door into a side room with the help of several soldiers. The walls of this side room are lined with portraits. Must be twenty of them – and every single one is Trujillo in a different ceremonial uniform. Does he come in here just so he can look at himself? Josh is still trying hold Satchel, who has not calmed down. El Presidente is fuming – Satch has ruined his frolic.

"Nobody told me nothin' about 10% of my dough getting jacked off the top," says Satch.

"I'm sure we can work this out..." says Aybar, but I'm not sure that's true.

"This is just the kind of jive we get back home – get offered one thing, show up, and get a big nasty surprise on payday. Uh uh, not this time. No how, no way."

"*Everyone* who is given the honor of working for the Dominican people tithes that amount," says Aybar. "They do it happily and proudly." Trujillo just stares at Satch, trying to size him up.

"That's *their* business, not *my* business. I'm in the *Satchel Paige business*, and *Satchel Paige wants to get paid what he was promised.*"

Before he can say another word, Josh addresses Aybar. "Just so I get this straight, you want us – as a group – to give back 10%. Of the $30,000."

"Just so," says Aybar. "As all Dominicans are asked to do. It is a donation to our great cause."

"Donation. Right," says Josh. "But if we *don't* donate..."

"It would show a grievous lack of gratitude," says Aybar. "The Exalted Benefactor might be forced to question his decision to bring you here. That might have....consequences."

That word – "consequences" – hangs in the air like a bad smell. We saw a lot of soldiers with a lot of guns on the way in here. "Okay," says Josh. "So there's no reason that Satch here can't cut himself a full slice of pie, and the rest of us get a tad less. As long as you get your three large."

Aybar looks at Trujillo, who looks at Josh, then at Satch, then back at Josh. Then he gives Aybar a tiny nod. "I believe," says Aybar, "that will satisfy El Presidente." Josh has saved the day.

"Okay then," says Josh.

"Excellent," says Aybar, smiling once again. "And now, since the first game is tomorrow at 1:00 p.m. and it is already 7:00 p.m., I suggest you gentlemen go to your hotel and get some rest. You must be weary from your journey."

"Suits me," says Satch. Never one to leave well enough alone, Satch sticks out his hand to Trujillo, who stares at it for a moment before gripping it. They shake. "No hard feelings, your Wonderfulship. Happy it worked out. Victory!"

We walk outside. The cool, balmy night air smells even sweeter. The limousines are gone, replaced by a line of taxis. Satch grabs the first one, and Josh and Cool Papa pile in with him. I grab the front seat, next to the driver.

"Take us to..." begins Josh.

"...the nastiest, loudest, gaudiest, wildest nightclub this town has got," says Satchel. Our driver grins and mashes down the gas pedal. We get thrown back in our seats as we chug off into the night.

CHAPTER FOURTEEN

We hear it before we can see it – that "bom bom, boo-dom boo-dom bah" drum-driven musical beat, almost like the flashy drummers they have in marching bands. Our driver smiles. "That, my friends, is MERENGUE!"

"Merengue?" asks Satch. "What's that?"

The driver gives him an "Are you crazy?" look in the rear view mirror. "Man, if you don't know merengue, you don't know *nothing*. Merengue is the sound of the Dominican. Merengue is the sound of HAPPINESS!" The cab jackrabbits to a stop in the middle of the street, because couples are dancing in front of the club. The fellas pile out and stare up at the showy red and green flashing neon sign – CLUB MOJITO. This place is jumping! They have these places in Pittsburgh they call "road houses" where musicians go after hours to cut loose and play rhythm and blues music so loud you can hear it a half a mile away. This place sounds like the rhythm without the blues. This merengue has got a beat that seems to get *inside* you. It dances you from the inside out!

We're ushered inside and the place is wall-to-wall party-hearty fun-lovers – exactly what Satchel asked for. I seen a lot of bands at the Crawford Grill – Count Basie, Earl Hines, Duke Ellington, Jimmie Lunceford – but I ain't NEVER seen a band that has more drummers than it does instrument players. This band has FOUR drummers – a regular drummer, two guys on conga drums, and a guy playing some kind of two-headed drum that he holds in his lap. He beats on one end with his hand and hits the other with a drumstick. There's also an accordion player and a guy playing an instrument I've never seen before – a wooden box with metal keys that he plucks. These cats are playing music that's loud, big, and happy, and the crowd jumps with every beat. The whole dance floor is a writhing sea of brown bodies decked out like a Dominican flag – red, green, and white.

The accordion player is the head man. He sees us standing at the door, and cuts off the band. Three huge spotlights swing over and blind us. He shouts, THE GODS OF BASEBALL ARE IN THE HOUSE!" and the whole place erupts in a joyous cheer, with whistles, hoots and shrieks mixed in for good measure. The band blasts out a fanfare, and three gigantic banners unfurl – painted pictures of Satch, Cool Papa, and Josh in their Dragones uniforms. More cheers. Women surge up from the crowd, grab the fellas and pull them onto the dance floor. Nova

Quezada, the glamour queen from the reception, grabs Satch, and he happily joins the celebration. Cool Papa laughs, and herds me over to a table just off the dance floor. Dr. Aybar pulls up a chair and joins us.

"Wild!" I say. It's like the club is a single dancing beast, and merengue is the heartbeat.

"The Great Benefactor loves merengue music, because it makes his people so happy," says Aybar. "I notice that Señor Paige can...what is the American expression...'cut a rug.'" Satchel has picked up the merengue moves in a flash, and is dancing with Nova Q. and two other young ladies. Josh is standing off to one side chatting with Julissa, that gal who sat next to him on the way to the rally. She's not wearing khaki fatigues now. She looks great in a raspberry red party dress with yellow flowers. Josh likes her, I can tell. She leads him onto the dance floor and shows him the steps. Imagine a cat teaching a grizzly bear how to fox trot – you get the picture.

"So Doc," says Cool Papa, "Got a question for you." Payday Thompson is now on stage, banging away on a conga drum. He's great, right on the beat.

"Certainly," says Dr. Aybar.

"It looks to me like El Presidente Trujillo runs a pretty tight ship here in the Dominican."

"Just so," says Aybar, gazing on the happy dancers.

"Statues everywhere, streets named after him – hell, the whole damn city is named after him. People shouting his name..."

"Dr. Trujillo is the heart and soul of the Dominican Republic," says Aybar. "He is beloved."

"Then why is it," says Cool Papa, leaning in so he doesn't have to shout over the music, "that he had to bring us over for these games? Games everybody keeps telling us we *have* to win? How could Trujillo possibly lose an election if everybody loves him, including God?"

Aybar shifts his gaze to Cool Papa. His smile straightens and his eyes harden. "Every great man faces great challenges. El Caudillo Trujillo is battling a shadowy network of evildoers hell-bent on defeating him, and enslaving the Dominican people. This group of depraved, villainous malefactors has no choice but to spread lies about our leader."

"Lies?" I say. "Like what?"

"These lies are so wicked – so despicable – that I would bring disgrace upon myself were I even to repeat them. Suffice it to say that they attribute to Dr. Trujillo monstrous crimes that, if true, would cause his people to denounce and shun him."

"So why can't Dr. Trujillo just tell the truth and that's that? Again, why bring *us* over? What does *baseball* have to do with any of this?" asks Cool Papa.

Now the smile returns to Dr. Aybar's face, but it's a thin smile, like my mama has when she wants me to understand the cold, hard facts of life. "I wish that politics were so simple," he says. "Alas, politics is as much about power as it is about truth. The Great Benefactor will demonstrate to our people that he is so powerful, he can conjure from thin air a baseball team that doesn't just defeat our adversaries. This team will be like a hammer that destroys them, humiliates them and, ultimately, eliminates them. Once that happens, El Caudillo can expose the source of the lies that have been created to bring him down, and bring the evil-doers to justice." Cool Papa leans back as he drinks in these words. Aybar takes a sip of his mojito and returns his gaze to the dance floor.

CRASH! The music stops mid-beat. Everybody – dancers, the band, and people at tables – look around, trying to figure out what just happened. Julissa is sprawled on the dance floor, with Josh standing just behind her. She's rubbing her cheek, with a shocked look on her face. Maximo Borgatti, Aybar's guy from the Klan fracas, is standing over her, heaving and staggering. He's drenched in sweat, wild eyes fixed on Julissa as he rubs his right fist. He's slugged her once. Now he looks like he's fixing to kill her. He's is in his army togs – is he here as a soldier? Could he arrest Josh and the fellas? Holy cow.

Julissa tries to stand, but Borgatti knocks her down again with a vicious backhanded slap to the face that knocks her out cold. Then he reaches around to the small of his back and pulls out a huge

Bowie knife, 15 inches at least. He takes a step toward her rag-doll body, but Josh steps over her, making his body a shield. Now it's Borgatti and his Bowie knife against Josh. "Don't," he says to Borgatti.

"She is my woman," says Borgatti. Woman? Like, wife?

"Back where I come from, a man don't pull a knife like that on *anybody*, 'specially a woman. Ain't done."

"Then why don't you go back where you came from? This doesn't concern you," says Borgatti.

"Does now," says Josh. He picks up one of the wooden chairs, which makes him look like a lion tamer in the circus. I look at Cool Papa, who looks back at me.

"Whaddaya think?" I ask.

"We've both seen Josh in worse scrapes than this," he replies. "But just in case, I hope you know how to play catcher." Dang! That's just about the only position I can't play.

Borgatti smiles an ice-cold smile, like a rattlesnake getting ready to strike. The two circle each other – Borgatti with the knife, Josh with the chair. The crowd forms a circle around them, turning the dance floor into a stage. The three spotlights focus on the two of them as they slow-dance around each other like Roman gladiators. Before I even know what's happening, Borgatti rears back and hurls the knife at

Josh. CRACK! Josh "catches" the knife in the wood brace of the chair bottom, the tip of the blade an inch from his heart. For a split second I think Josh has him, and so does Josh. He pulls the knife out of the chair and looks at Borgatti...who has pulled a chrome-plated derringer out of his boot. He points it right at Josh, who keeps circling him with the knife.

The other ballplayers have gathered around Josh, and some soldiers circle behind Borgatti. This has every sign of turning into the kind of brawl where people die, and we ain't even played a single inning yet. I see a dead-eyed look on Bogatti's face, and I am absolutely sure that he's going to shoot Josh in the chest. Then, BANG! A gunshot splits the air. Where did that come from? I whip around and see Dr. Aybar standing, holding a smoking pistol. He's just fired a single shot into the ceiling of the nightclub. As usual, he's perfectly composed, and this seems to calm everyone down. It certainly gets our attention.

Aybar slides the pistol back in the holster of the young soldier standing next to him, and says, "This, my friends, is a celebration." He turns and looks at Borgatti. "Our beloved patron, the one who has brought these men here for the greater glory of the Dominican, El Caudillo – he would be most unhappy if you, er, 'accidentally' killed one of our star players on the eve of the first game." Borgatti is still facing Josh. No one in the club moves a muscle. Then, very slowly, Borgatti lowers the derringer. Josh brings down the knife. Borgatti puts the weapon back in his boot and walks away. The crowd scatters back into the club. Josh picks Julissa off the floor. She's still out cold. He walks her body to the door of the club and lays her on the white canvas stretcher carried by the two fellas from the ambulance. As Josh watches them carry her away, Dr. Aybar comes up to Cool Papa.

"Señor Bell," says Dr. Aybar, "A word of advice. Your friend and colleague Josh Gibson has just performed a great deed of chivalry." Borgatti and Josh are still staring at each other, neither willing to be the first to look away. "In doing so," continues Aybar, "he has shamed Señor Borgatti in front of this crowd, and in front of his woman. Señor Borgatti will almost certainly seek revenge."

"Revenge?" asks Cool Papa. Aybar nods. "What's your advice, Doc?"

"Tell him that Señor Borgatti is a trusted servant of Dr. Trujillo. As part of that service, Borgatti kills men and has them killed. He does this without regret or even a second thought. In fact, I believe that he has come to…well…enjoy it. Warn Señor Gibson that Señor Borgatti will nurture this grudge, and will seek an opportunity to confront him. Tell Josh to watch himself, and be ready. And now, please join me." Our waiter arrives with a tray of mojitos and puts them down in front of us just as Josh returns.

"Compliments of the house," says the waiter as Cool Papa tries to pay.

"Well," says Josh, "hope I didn't spoil the party." He picks up his drink and sips. His hand is trembling. I look at Cool Papa. We're both thinking of what Aybar said. Should we tell Josh? The look on Josh's face tells us both that he already knows.

CHAPTER FIFTEEN

The fellas are giddy as they pile out of the taxis in front of our hotel. They're still singing and dancing and cutting up. Yeah, they are a bit tipsy, but that's because the people in the club kept buying them drinks and asking them to tell stories about baseball back in the U.S.. All that happy chatter fades out when the guys look at our hotel – if this IS our hotel.

The Hotel Trujillo Palacio Grande looks like an even bigger, even grander eight-story version of Trujillo's presidential digs. You have to walk up a huge marble stairway just to get to the revolving doors. Halfway up the stairs, there's Trujillo himself – at least a gold statue of him, dressed as a General, sitting on a horse, and pointing a sword at the sky. The statue is in the middle of a big fountain with eight water geysers. As we stand there, a bunch of people brush past us heading into the hotel. They are all white people. Little Willie Tatum breaks the silence. "You absolutely *sure* this is our hotel?"

"Trujillo Palacio Grande," says Cool Papa, checking the paper that Dr. Aybar gave him. Cool Papa doesn't move, just looks up at this fortress. Everyone turns to look at Satch. What's he going to do?

"Never saw a hotel this fancy didn't have a big ol' sign over the front door sayin' 'No Coloreds.'"

"Peanut!" That's Josh. He's got a look on his face – the one he gets when the game is on the line, and he's made his mind up to get a hit. "Grab my grip." He's toting his bag of bats. I get his suitcase. He starts up the steps, two at a time. I shadow him. He doesn't even stop to look at the statue. He just vaults right around it. Now we're standing at the entrance. A beefy black bellman stands between us and the front door. He doesn't step aside, just stares at Josh. "Drop the bag, Peanut." I put it down in front of the bellman, who keeps staring at Josh.

"You…you are the American. Gibson."

"That's right," says Josh."

"The king of home runs. Here to lead us to…victory," says the bellman, saying the last word as if it were "heaven" or "promised land."

"Right again," says Josh. He's still not used to being recognized so far from home. The bellman grabs his hand and yanks his whole arm up and down, like a thirsty farmer working a water pump. Josh breaks into a big grin, but after a while he doesn't know what to do – the bellman won't let go. Finally Josh puts his hand on the man's shoulder, freezing the pump. The bellman lets go, and grabs the bag on the ground. He slides the bats off of Josh's shoulder onto his own, and walks inside the hotel. Josh turns, grinning, and waves at the other guys, who race up the steps and stride proudly into that hotel lobby like it's the most natural thing in the world.

I think back on that shabby fleabag back in Alabama, where we practically got killed just for trying to register. This hotel is as luxurious as that place was dumpy. And the rooms! I'm Josh's roommate, and our room not only has big soft beds with clean, crispy white sheets, it has its own bathroom. I never seen anything this deluxe, except for Gus Greenlee's place on the third floor of the Crawford Grille, where he has the same deal – an office with a bathroom that has a bath and a shower, like this place here.

Josh takes a shower and then I get in there and take a nice, long, relaxing soak in that gigantic cast-iron claw foot bathtub. That thing is so big it takes twenty minutes to fill up, and I can practically swim in it, like the Highland Park Plunge back in Pittsburgh. And, of course, here I don't have to worry about getting beat up for sticking my toe in the water.

Josh is in bed when I get out, but he's not asleep yet. He's staring at the ceiling. "What're you thinking about?" I ask.

"Nothing. Just the usual," he says softly. 'Bout life. What it is, what I want, stuff like that."

"I know what *I* want," I say.

"Really? And what might that be?" says Josh.

"I want to be *rich*. I want to be richer than Gus Greenlee, so's I can buy Mama a big house and a car with a chauffeur and I can have my own baseball team." Josh snorts loudly, then hoots with laughter. "What?"

"Only gents I know can rub two nickels together are Gus Greenlee and Satchel Paige. Either one of them strike you has happy?"

Never thought of that. "Well…no…"

"'Course not. Happiness don't come from money once you got enough to live. Happiness, that comes from something else."

"Which is?"

"Not sure you'd understand."

"You could try me. I'm pretty smart," I say.

"Not smart enough to stay outta trouble," he says, smiling at me.

"Smart enough to have you as a friend so I don't *need* to stay outta trouble." He laughs at this.

"Okay, okay. I figure happiness comes from having some kind of special…*something*, you know? God's gift, that he gives us to make other people happy. Like, look at Satchel. God made him like a whip, so he can sling a baseball with more locomotion than anybody else, drive the fans crazy. And God made me in a certain way too."

"Big and strong," I say.

"Yeah, that, but there's a *lot* of guys who are big and strong. He made me...how can I put this..." He stops, thinks. "You ever see Louie Armstrong play the trumpet?"

"Yeah, sure, at the Grille."

"What makes him special? Lot of trumpeters play like Gabriel, but he's the Trumpet *King*. Why?" I never thought of it till right now.

"I dunno. He can hit those high notes..." I say.

"Lot of guys can hit high notes. It's not the notes, it's the *feelin'*. When I watch Louie, I can *feel* the joy that he feels playing that horn. That's why I go see him, 'cuz when he plays, I get that same happy feelin.'"

"Yeah, that's right," I say.

"God made Louie to play that horn to make people happy. That's what I feel playin' baseball. God made me to stand up there at home plate and face down that pitcher and hit that baseball so far that people will feel the pleasure I get in doin' it."

"Yeah!" I say.

"Only...."

"Only what?"

"Only here's where I get confused. 'Cuz that same God gave me black skin."

"Me too," I say.

"So if God made me to play this game and hit that ball and make people feel happy, why did he give me black skin?"

"Well..." I say, trying to think of an answer. Only I can't.

"In New York they got a stadium holds 60,000 people. Can you imagine what it'd be like to play ball in front of 60,000 folks? I feel like that's what God made me for, but I can't even buy a decent seat in that stadium! I can't do it because I'm black. Don't make no sense to me." He's right. Finally I say something just to break up the hush in the room.

"Maybe, " I say, "this whole thing here in the Dominican is s'posed to change all that. Maybe when you win this series it'll get reported in all the papers, and Mister Griffith'll see what a mistake he made. Maybe God's just making you wait a little bit, so it'll make playing in the big leagues all the sweeter." Josh doesn't say anything. I can tell he don't believe me.

"G'night, Peanut. Thanks for what you said. Hope it's true. Now go to sleep." And with that he turns out the lights.

October 12, 1937

CRASH!

What was that? Sounded like a lamp hitting the floor. More clatter. What time is it? Pitch dark in the room. Now a light goes on, in the bathroom. Alarm clock says 2:00 a.m. Where's Josh? He's not in bed. Somebody's in the bathroom. Is it him? He stumbles out and I close my eyes like I'm still sleeping. He's trying to walk on tiptoes but the more he tries to be quiet, the more racket he kicks up. He's all dressed up as he heads out the door. He told my mama he'd take care of me, but I've gotta look out for him too. The second he shuts the door I toss off the covers, throw on my clothes and shadow him.

Even at 2:00 a.m. the air here smells sweet – sweet and cool and soft. Josh never looks backwards so I don't have any trouble trailing him as he walks the five blocks from the Rafael Trujillo Hotel to the Rafael Trujillo Hospital, at the corner of Exalted Leader Avenue and Benefactor of the Fatherland Drive. He slips inside. I see him dodge the lobby and start up some stairs. He walks up to the 3rd floor. When I open the same door, a huge fist grabs my shirt and I'm nose to nose with a very angry face. "You're s'posed to be in the *sack*, Peanut."

"So are you," I squeak back at him.

"I got business here."

"I can help you."

"No you can't. Now *git*." I don't move. What's he going to do? Drag me five blocks, kicking and screaming? "Peanut..."

"You're here to see that girl, aren't you?" His eyes flash, and I know I'm right.

"Look," he says, "you can stay if you wait outside the room. Only gonna be a minute, just want to make sure she's okay."

"Deal," I say. I follow him to Room 311. Josh knocks. No answer. He opens the door and walks inside. I grab it before it shuts so I can get a better listen. Pause, then a light goes on.

"Hey," says Josh. "Hope I didn't wake you."

"No. I was awake. Thinking. Thank you."

"For what?" asks Josh.

"Tonight. You saved my life."

"Naw..."

"Yes, you did. Maximo, he...he would have killed me."

"What's Borgatti got on you?"

"You don't want to know."

"Look, the guy hates me anyway," says Josh. "Even before that fight..."

"Why?"

"No idea. So why was he trying to kill you?"

"Because he is Lucifer, the fallen angel of the Bible. He wants everyone around him to cower in fear."

"Why?"

"He is Trujillo's clenched fist, the head of the SIM, our Exalted Benefactor's personal army. My father's secret police." Uh oh. *My father...*

"You *father*? You sayin'...." Nobody says anything for a long time. Then Julissa speaks in a loud whisper.

"Before he became El Presidente, Señor Trujillo was a soldier. He had many affairs, including one with my mother. She was a waitress and dancer at a merengue club."

"So that's why...that's what you were doin' when you met us as we got off the plane? You did it for your father?"

"I'm making a film about him. About these games."

"What kind of film?" She chuckles.

"A film to tell the world of his 'greatness'."

"Not sure I understand…"

"My father idolizes the Chancellor of Germany, Herr Hitler. Hitler had Leni Riefenstahl make a movie about him, called Triumph of the Will."

"Never heard of it," says Josh. Julissa laughs.

"It is what they call 'propaganda.' A film to make the world fear and revere Hitler. If Herr Hitler has a film, so must my father, so the world will fear and worship him."

"Are you afraid of him?"

"Trujillo?" She laughs. "Are you?"

"No. Well, yeah. I guess. He's my boss," says Josh.

"Everyone is scared of him. Except me."

"Why not you?" asks Josh.

"Whoever you fear owns you. Nobody owns me."

"Should I be scared of him?"

"Not if you win your baseball games," say Julissa.

"Dang!" says Josh, raising his voice for the first time. "Everybody keeps tellin' us that."

"Because it's true," she says.

"Okay, so what if we *don't* win?"

"Then," says Julissa, "you will find yourself face to face with a man who is unfettered by ideas of right and wrong. An evil man."

"Evil?"

"A man who forced me to watch as a firing squad murdered my mother. " The words hit me like a fist in the stomach. I can't breathe.

"What?" says Josh, his voice a hoarse whisper.

"In a prison courtyard."

"No...."

"By Maximo Borgatti. And then my father, the Great Benefactor, forced me, at gunpoint, to marry Señor Borgatti, because Borgatti wanted me, and what I wanted didn't matter. That's your boss, Señor Gibson."

Holy cow. What have I gotten myself into??? Nobody says anything for a real long time. Finally, Josh says, "So Borgatti..."

"Still thinks he owns me, but that's no longer true. And as long as my father thinks my film can make him worshipped and feared the world over, then Borgatti can't do a thing."

"I came here 'cuz I thought you might need me. Turns out *I'm* the one who needs *you*."

"You need to go get some sleep. You and your friend, behind the door there." Oops. Josh grabs me and yanks me into the room. I see Julissa for the first time. The whole left side of her face is covered with a white gauze bandage. She shakes my hand, and turns back to Josh. "You need to win today's game. You must be careful. I will help you all I can, but there's only so much I can do."

"Thanks." He leans over and kisses her forehead.

"This place is trouble."

"I can handle Borgatti."

"He is only one of your worries."

"What else is there?"

"Win your games, and you'll never find out. Lose them, and..."

"And what?"

"And you may not live to find out."

CHAPTER SIXTEEN

Trujillo Field. Most of our guys are talkin' low and movin' slow, hung over after a full evening of alcoholic festivities at the Club Mojito. But they're relaxed. The general way of thinking is that this is going to be a pick-up game against a gaggle of wide-eyed locals. "I could fall outta bed at 3:00 a.m. and beat these chumps with my worst stuff" is how Satch puts it when Cool Papa asks him how he feels. "Satchel is here to have fun, and to show these gazooneys how *real* baseball is played." A gazooney is a guy who puts up the tent when the carnival comes to town. Satch isn't worried about losing, that's for sure. Josh frowns at him. He's using a bone to rub down his bats. He's not hung over, just tired. Don't think he's quite so sure we're gonna win.

I'm right beside Josh as the Crawfords walk from the dressing room into the dugout and then onto the field...and my whole body goes all goose bumpy. We're right in the middle of 40,000 standing-and-screaming, pennant-waving baseball crazies – "Los

Fanaticos Locos." Our guys just stand there and look at them. Imagine the Mardi Gras, the World Series, and a Presidential Inauguration all happening at once, and Julissa's newsreel cameras catch it all.

The fans are only a part of it. A forty piece merengue-style marching band in red and blue uniforms – six drummers, four guys on congas, four accordion players, plus saxes, trumpets, trombones, tubas, clarinets, and marimbas – is pumping out high-octane party music. The outfield fence, both dugouts, and the foul lines are covered with red and blue bunting and huge banners that read, "Re-Elect The Great Benefactor," with big pictures of Trujillo's stony face.

Then, just like at the rally, the band blares out a fanfare fit for royal coronation. The racket from the stands stops dead, and every eye in the park turns to a box right behind first base. Here comes El Presidente Trujillo himself, dressed in his flashy white military get-up, followed by his wife, kids, Borgatti, couple other bodyguard types, and Dr. Aybar, in his ice cream suit. Behind them are a couple hundred soldiers, who fan out in the stands to keep the crazies from starting a riot. There's Julissa with that Eyemo camera in her hands. She's shooting Trujillo and yelling at her other camera guys to follow her lead. Trujillo strolls to his "throne" – a special gold plated ceremonial chair with a red velvet seat that's raised up so he can see better (and everyone can see him). He examines the crowd like he's the Principal, it's the first day of school, and he wants to scope out the troublemakers. Then he smiles and waves, and the whole place erupts in a joyful whoop.

Now the guys are loosening up, playin' pepper, and doing wind sprints. I see Josh and Cool Papa look into the stands, and they aren't happy. I walk over. "What's up?"

"You remember that guy from the plane? White dude, gaudy shirt? What was his name?" asks Josh.

I remember him real well. "Tyler Underwood," I say.

"Look over there," he says. He's pointing to a box on the third base side. There's Underwood, surrounded by a bunch of guys who look just like him – middle-age, white, flashy shirts, big drinks in one hand and bags of peanuts in the other, laughing and clowning. The box looks like a slab of angel food cake in the middle of huge box of chocolates.

"So what?" I say. Guy said he was a baseball fan.

"So nothing," says Josh. "Pretty fancy box for a fan, even a big shot."

Another blast of music tells everyone that game time has arrived. I'm between Satch and Josh as our guys line up along the third base line. The other team runs out on the field for the first time. As the San Pedro de Macoris Sugar Kings line up in front of first base, I see Satch's jawbone drop off his face and hit the dirt in front of him. He stares at the other guys like they're Confederate dead come to re-fight the

Civil War. "Lord have mercy. Do you fellas see what Satchel sees?"

"I see it," says Cool Papa, "but I don't believe it." The fans stand up as the merengue marching band plays "Valiant Quisqueyans," the Dominican National Anthem.

"Those sonsabitches done brought in *Cubans*!" says Satch. Cubans? The Sugar Kings don't look like "gazooneys" – the punch-and-judy locals we were expecting. These guys look like *our* guys – big, muscular, and confident. They're loosey-goosey, like they know they're going to win.

"Ain't that Showboat Sanchez?" asks Josh, nodding toward a particularly big, black, mean-looking Sugar King.

"Almost took Satch's head off with a line drive last year," says Satch, his voice raspy with shock.

"And that's Crush Coleman," says Cool Papa, "the shortstop almost beat me in a footrace down in Havana..."

"And I'll be damned if that ain't Louie Ramos, and Pablo Marcel and Choo-Choo Diaz," says Josh.

"Dang! Lookee there! Tell me that's not who I think it is," says Satch, pointing at the very last player standing in line. Josh and Cool Papa see what Satch sees, and both players look like they been hit with a shovel.

"Marty Dihigo," says Josh.

"Oh man oh man oh man," mutters Cool Papa.

"What's the big deal?" I ask Josh.

"Game down in Havana two years ago," says Josh, still staring at him. "Dihigo versus Satchel. Satchel pitches a one-hitter and loses, because Dihigo throws a no-hitter."

"Wow," I say.

"And guess who got the one hit," says Cool Papa. "A monster home run, off Satchel's best fastball."

"Dihigo?" I ask, as I stare at the man himself.

"Bingo," says Cool Papa.

"Hells bells," says Satch, "They went and got themselves a *damn Cuban All-Star team!*" As the Dominican anthem bounces to climax, Satch walks over to Cool Papa Bell. "They can't *do* this to ol' Satch."

Before he can answer, the plate umpire yells, "Play ball!" Satch ignores him.

"Man, they can't do this to ol' Satch! They done brought in a damn bunch of ringers!" I've never seen Satch so discombobulated.

"Satch," says Josh from behind Cool Papa, "WE'RE ringers."

"Okay, yeah, maybe," admits Satch. "But…well, dang, this was supposed to be a cakewalk. I came here to *party*!"

"Game time," says Josh, looking dead serious. "Let's play us some catch. We can beat these guys." But Satch can't seem to shake this sudden case of nerves.

"Dang!" he says, pacing in a circle.

"PLAY…BALL!!!" the Umpire yells again, this time right at Satch. Satch starts walking toward the umpire like he's gonna beef him about the Cubans when Josh grabs him by both arms and spins him around so they are nose to nose.

"SATCH!" he screams right in Satch's face. This finally snaps him out of his downward spiral.

"What?"

"You keep tellin' me you're the greatest player in baseball. ARE YOU?" asks Josh.

"Yeah, of course!" says Satch.

"Then PROVE IT!" says Josh, spinning Satch around and pushing him toward the pitcher's mound. Then he trots back toward home plate. The Umpire throws Satch a pearly white ball. Crush Coleman steps in, and we have ourselves a ballgame.

Funny thing about baseball. You put two great teams on the field, and it all comes down to who goofs up the least. Take Satch. I don't know if it was the booze or merengue-dancing all night or all those cigars he smoked or general overconfidence, but his fastball doesn't have the "pop" that makes everyone so scared of him. What's worse, he can't hit his spots. His heater is two inches off the black part of the plate instead of one, and the Cubans hit line drives all over the diamond. Every time the Sugar Kings hit another frozen rope I look at El Presidente Trujillo. He looks dismal, like a rich kid at a birthday party who didn't get the pony he was promised.

And it isn't just Satchel. Ground balls that Willie Tatum vacuums up in his sleep flick off the tip of his glove. Out in centerfield, Cool Papa muffs a fly ball he'd usually catch in his back pocket. But even with our guys struggling and the Cubans playing their best, the Cubans are only up 7 to 4 in the bottom of the 9th. Louie Ramos has been throwing beebees all day, and he quickly strikes out Flash Fowler and Bullet Hampton. I steal a glance at Trujillo – he's seething. He's pacing up and down in front of his throne, barking at Borgatti, who is listening and nodding.

Then we get a break. Cool Papa Bell fouls off eleven pitches to work Ramos for a walk. Deacon Powell pops a perfect bunt single up the first base line that Ramos bobbles. Base hit, Cool Papa advancing to third. Then Ramos hits Payday Thompson in the elbow with a screwball. Winning runs on base, and Josh Gibson coming to bat. All day long the stands have been jumpin' as "Los Fanaticos Locos" have cheered, jeered, groaned, and passed silver coins back and forth, laying down bets on every single pitch. Now a hush falls over the crowd. Everyone knows what's at stake. Our fellas were brought over to win. It's winnin' time.

Josh is one for four – a double in 3rd inning – as he steps in. He plants his right foot, then his left. Then he rolls up his left sleeve to show off that knot of home run muscle, and glares at Ramos. If he's tuckered out from the night before he sure doesn't show it. I can see sweat dripping off Ramos, but he doesn't wipe his brow. He winds up and whips a fastball low and outside. Ball one. Josh backs out, but doesn't look for a sign. He's up there looking for a fastball so he can end this thing with a dinger. Now Ramos is winding up again. The pitch is a ferocious heater, letter-high and inside – Josh's meat and potatoes. Josh rips it – CRACK! – and the ball takes off like a rocket toward left center field.

The fans leap up, tracking that ball as it arcs toward the fence. The Sugar Kings' center fielder, Cookie Valdez, has taken off at a dead run at the crack of the bat. Back..back...back... Cool Papa is already across home plate and Deacon Powell has rounded third. Josh is still standing at home plate, eyes fixed on the ball. I wave my hands, trying to help the ball over the fence. It's *got* to clear that fence! I'm sure it's over when Valdez does something I've never seen a ballplayer do before or since. He doesn't crash into the fence, or leap up in front of it. He runs smack into Trujillo's re-election poster pasted on the fence, plants his right foot on Trujillo's nose, and vaults himself five feet in the air, like a circus acrobat. He shoots his right hand straight up into the air. THWACK! It's an "ice cream cone" – ball perched at the very top of the fingers of his glove, like a scoop of tutti-frutti. Then he crash lands back on earth, does a full forward roll on the outfield grass – and holds up the glove. He's got it! DANG!

The high-pitched shriek of the fans drops down into a death gargle groan. Trujillo's mouth drops open. Then he whirls and pokes Borgatti in the chest, like Borgatti's the one who blew the game. Julissa turns away and pulls her index finger across her throat – CUT! Her cameramen stop shooting. El Presidente is royally cheesed off, and she doesn't want this on film. The Cubans mob Valdez, grabbing him at home plate, hoisting him on their shoulders and carrying him off the field. Our guys trudge off the field – all except Josh, who is still standing at home holding his bat. If Josh catches that horsehide one-hundredth of an inch lower, it's 200 feet over the fence. Instead, well – as Josh says when he hands me his bat, "Just another damn can o' corn."

I been to three funerals in my life, and none of them were as gloomy as our locker room. All the fellas are moping around as I gather up the gear and stuff it in the equipment bags, and then we all pile back on the "Victory Express" bus that drove us to the ballpark. Dr. Aybar stands next to the door as we get in. He ain't smilin' now. He scowls. Borgatti is the bus driver, and he looks angrier than Aybar. Once we're on the bus, Aybar sits up front next to Borgatti.

"Hey, we'll get 'em next time," says Cool Papa.

"Damn, damn, damn, damn, damn," says Josh, head in his hands. He's taking it hard.

"Just one game," says Satchel.

"Is that what you think?" asks Aybar, sharply.

"Yeah, that's what I think," says Satch. "Next time Satchel won't be surprised to see them Cubans. Next time I'll be ready."

"Did you hear what the Great Benefactor said about losing?" asks Aybar.

"Sayin' it is one thing, Doc. Not doin' it is something else entirely. The Great Benefactor never tried to sneak a fastball by Martin Dihigo when he was hung over," says Satch.

"I believe our beloved leader urged you to go back to your hotel and get some rest instead of carousing all night," says Aybar. This makes Satch mad.

"So what's El Presidente gonna do about it, Doc? He gonna make us take extra batting practice? He gonna fire us and bring in the New York Yankees? He ain't gonna do a damn thing except let us win the next game."

"I....I wouldn't be so sure about that," says Cool Papa, staring out his window. Everyone on the bus turns to look at him.

"What do you mean?" asks Josh.

"This ain't the way back to the hotel," says Cool Papa. I look out my window. We've left the city. Fields of sugar cane are whizzing by us. Something's up and whatever it is gives me a real bad feeling in the pit of my stomach.

CHAPTER SEVENTEEN

I'm scared stiff. What's happening? I look at Josh. He looks back. He can read my mind.

"Remember what I told your mama?" he asks. His voice is low, serious.

"You...told her you'd look after me."

"Have I done that so far?"

"Yeah?"

"Ain't nothin' changed since then," he says.

I can see something looming up over the fields of sugar cane. Looks like a fortress, or an abandoned castle. The closer we get, the scarier it gets. "Where you takin' us?" asks Satchel. Aybar doesn't answer.

"Looks like some kind of fort. Or maybe...a prison," says Cool Papa.

"Just so," says Aybar without turning around. I remember what Julissa said about Trujillo and Borgatti and what happened to her mama.

"Josh. They don't put people in jail for playin' ball, do they?" asks Satchel under his breath, so Aybar can't hear.

"Not for playin'. Just for losin'," says Josh.

A thirty-foot high rusted iron gate groans open and the bus lurches inside, then stops. Borgatti cranks the door open, jumps off the bus, and screams at us to get off. Josh is the second one off the bus. I'm the third, just behind him. It's a prison, all right – a dank, mean-looking medieval fortress of rough gray stone, with walls that loom over us like the wings of a huge, evil dragon.

A Guardia Nacional uses the silver bayonet on his rifle to shove me up against a pockmarked, freestanding red brick wall in the middle of this courtyard. I'm between Satch and Josh. The other fellas get pushed into line as they get off the bus. This is a dang firing squad! "Peanut," whispers Josh, "*remember what I said on the bus.*" He's the only one who isn't petrified. He's got that look of cool defiance he gets when he's up against the very best pitchers, like Satch or Dizzy Dean.

Now we're backed against the wall. Payday Thompson is wobbly-kneed and whimpering, and Little Willie Tatum actually starts cryin' as the soldiers square up in front us, rifles at their sides. Borgatti barks some kind of command and the door to a prison office swings open. El President Trujillo struts out in a new outfit – khaki green army fatigues. The ceremonial sword is gone – now he's got a gaudy chrome-plated military pistol on his hip. He strides over to the line up, and looks us over. Then he pulls the pistol from its holder and points it straight up in the air.

"¡LISTOS!" The soldiers, as one, bring their guns up into firing position.

"Oh, man..." says Cool Papa

"This ain't happenin'," mutters Satch.

"Take it easy," murmurs Josh, drawing out the last word – "eaaazzzzzzy."

"Easy?" says Satch, amazed.

"The Great Benefactor has one damn chance to win this thing, and it ain't by croakin' us," says Josh.

"How you know he ain't got Dizzy Dean and Joe DiMaggio stashed in some hotel?" says Satch. Trujillo stabs the air with his pistol, thrusting it straight up.

"¡APUNTEN!" The Guardia Nacionals shoulder their rifles, sighting us down their rifle barrels. I can see which soldier is aimed at which player. Third from the right has a bead on my forehead.

"He ain't got nobody stashed nowhere," says Josh. "This is a bluff to scare us to death."

"It's workin'," says Cool Papa.

Trujillo lowers his arm, but the soldiers don't stand down – they're still in firing position, fingers curved on triggers. El President walks right in front of us. He stops to look Satch in the eye, then Cool Papa, and finally Josh. Josh is the only one who isn't shivering like it's 20 below zero. As he stares at Josh, I get a good look at Trujillo's face, and something clicks in. His face is a lighter shade of brown than his neck – the opposite of most folks. He's wearing make-up! Like my Mama puts on before she goes to work. He's whitened his face. Whew, that's really weird.

Luckily, he doesn't catch me staring at him. Trujillo jumps back and swivels his head so he takes in the whole team. Then he screams at the top of his lungs, "EL...PRESIDENTE...NO...PIERDE!" He thrusts his hand in the air. "¡FUEGO!" He fires his pistol, and a split second later the air explodes with an ear-splitting crack of thunder as the rifleman let fly.

I'm hit! Ain't I? I feel a sharp pain, but it's in my arm – Josh has grabbed me. I suddenly realize that I'm screaming my head off. I stop when I see his face – smiling through the rifle smoke. I look around. Everyone's still alive. The rifle barrels of the Guardia Nacionals are aimed about an inch over our heads. The firing squad missed on purpose, to scare the daylights out of us.

The smoke clears. There's Trujillo, pistol at his side, glaring at us. He executes a crisp military about-face and marches off. The soldiers march off behind him, leaving us with Dr. Aybar.

"Gentlemen," he says, "If you should lose another ballgame, especially in the manner this one was lost – because of sluggishness due to dissipation – you will once again find yourself face to face with these young patriots, and they won't be firing over your heads. You will now be returned to your hotel. I *strongly* suggest you get a good night's sleep, and prepare yourself for tomorrow's game."

CHAPTER EIGHTEEN

I know I'm supposed to be asleep, but I can't sleep. I'm lyin' on the bed staring at the ceiling, thinking about what happened. I could be dead! Just like that! It never occurred to me that I could get snuffed and it'd be all over before my life even got started. "Josh," I whisper. I figure he's asleep, but I want to be sure.

"Go to sleep, Peanut."

"You awake?" I ask.

"How could I talk and sleep at the same time?" Good question. "Now go to sleep."

"Can't sleep. All I can think of is those soldiers. Do you really think they woulda shot us?" I hear him roll over, and then I see his face on the pillow, lookin' over at me.

"No way that was gonna happen," he says.

"You were the only guy on the team had it figured that way. Why was that?" Josh realizes I'm too buzzed up from the day's events to sack out. He sits up in bed and turns the lamp on that's on the table between our beds.

"I knew we were okay as soon as I saw Trujillo himself. He's a bully, like Gus Greenlee. He has to make a big show of everything. He just wanted to scare the daylights out of us. If he wanted to kill us, he would have had Borgatti pull the bus over to the side of the road, stood us front of a ditch and shot us in the back of the head."

"How'd you know that?"

"Just made sense."

"Is that why you weren't scared?"

"Oh, I was scared all right."

"But you didn't show it."

"Let me tell you somethin', Peanut. Everybody's scared of some damn thing, but you always got a choice. You can let it get you, or decide that you're bigger than it is."

"How do you do that?" I ask.

"Tell you what I do. The most scared I ever was in my life is when I was nineteen years old. I'd just gotten married, and my wife – her name was Helen, Helen Mason – she was gonna have twins. I'd just signed my first baseball contract, with the Homestead Grays. Got my first uniform. Hit my first home run. It was like God was giving me everything I wanted, all at one time. And then..." He stopped talking, and just stared off into space.

"And then what?"

"Got a call at the ballpark one day. Helen was in the hospital, she'd gone into premature labor. Took a taxi over there. Ran up to her room. She'd had the twins – a boy and a girl, but something had gone wrong, and she…she was….” He stops. I look over at him, and see tears rolling down his cheeks. Never seen him cry before.

“She was…” I try to help him a little.

“Dead,” he whispers. “Good lord had taken her. 19 years old. She was gone. Poor Helen. Never loved any woman….” He stops again, then sniffs and sits up straight. “You want to talk about ‘scared’, Peanut? I’d gotten a taste of my future – playin’ ball, getting’ paid, makin’ people cheer and shout. People were payin’ good money to see me live out my dream, only now I had these two babies. What was I supposed to do? Quit baseball and spend 18 years – my whole life as a ballplayer – to raise ‘em up? Go back to Gimbel’s Department Store and run that damn elevator the rest of my life?” I didn’t say anything for a long time.

“So what did you do?” I finally ask.

“I couldn’t figure out why God was doin’ this to me. I could either give up the thing he made me for and lose my reason for bein’ alive, or I could play ball and give up my kids. What would YOU do, Peanut?”

“I dunno,” I say. Scares me just to hear about it. Can’t imagine making a choice like that.

“Helen’s folks offered to take the kids. Named the girl Helen after her mother. Boy’s name is Josh Junior. I see ‘em when I’m in town, which is about 2 months a year.” He stares at the ceiling for a long time. “I’m not really their father, just a guy who comes around once in a while and brings ‘em stuff.” Josh puts his head in his hands and rubs his eyes. “I did the wrong thing, Peanut. I shoulda given up baseball, brought up those kids myself. I had a responsibility.” I start to say something, but stop. The man’s in pain. Better to let him work it out. “I always figured,” he continues, his voice raspy now, “that someday, maybe, somethin’ would come along where I could make up for what I did. The same chance, only different. Where I could stand up and do the *right* thing.”

“Like today. Like the firing squad. Everybody could see you were the only one who wasn’t afraid. Kept the other guys from losing it,” I say.

“Yeah, I guess,” he says. “But that was a little thing. There’s something else going on here. People actin’ crazy, but maybe it ain’t so crazy if we knew what it was all about. I got a feeling that we’re gonna find out what’s really goin’ on. Maybe that’ll be my chance. Hope I’ll be ready this time.”

“You will be,” I say.

“Maybe,” he says. “Hope so. Now go back to sleep. Gotta win tomorrow, no ifs ands or buts.”

CHAPTER NINETEEN

October 13, 1937

Dear Mama,

How are you? I am fine. Hope this letter gets to you. Cool Papa helped me figure out how to send it "Air Mail Special Delivery" so you won't have to wait six months or anything.

I wish you were here with us. The weather is fine, and the people are very friendly.

(Except, of course, for the members of that firing squad.)

We lost the first game, but I think we have a good chance to win the second one, because now the guys are used to the climate and how they play down here.

(I certainly hope we win, because if we lose, there won't be a third game, as we'll all be dead.)

Josh is looking after me just fine, and I am learning all kinds of new things.

(Like what a mojito tastes like, how to do the merengue, and what it means to do the right thing even when the other guy has a knife.)

I will write more soon. Bus is about to leave for the ballpark. I love you, Mama.

With love, from your Clyde.

Next game is different. The fellas are sober, focused and all business. First time I can remember that nobody says a word on the bus to the game, or in the locker room, or standing on the base line as they play the Dominican national anthem. No woofin', no razzin', no horseplay, no nothing. As Cool Papa Bell steps in to lead off the top of the first, I see Trujillo nod to Borgatti from his first base throne. Borgatti is stationed in our dugout, with three of his biggest, nastiest Guardia Nacionals next to him in full combat regalia, with bandoleers of machine gun bullets slung across their chests. All three were in our personal firing squad, and they all look like they're eager for a second chance.

This game is a classic pitcher's duel, played out under a blazing Dominican sun. Satch is our guy, and today he's a demon – unstoppable. He's painting the black part of the plate with a lightning fastball that has the Cubans tied up in knots. The Cubans throw Lefty Tiant at us, and he's just the opposite of Satch. He throws nothing but junk – lazy curves, changeups, slow screwballs and every kind of doctored pitch you can think of – spitball, shine ball, and emery ball. The only time he throws a fastball is to knock one of our fellas down, which he does every single inning. In the first eight innings, Satch gives up two walks and no hits. Lefty Tiant hits three guys (including Josh twice), gives up five walks and seven hits, including a leadoff triple to Willie Tatum in the fifth. Lucky for Tiant he's got a wicked pickoff move – he catches three of our guys leaning the wrong way, including Tatum, who was dead set on stealing home.

So now it's the 9th inning, zero to zero. Martin Dihigo stands in. I know Satch – he figures he's got his no-hitter in the bag. When he does that, he starts doggin' it. He almost always wastes the first pitch just to see if the batter is over-eager, but this time he tries to sneak a fastball past their best hitter, and the big man blasts it up the alley in right field. By the time the dust settles Dihigo is on third, Satchel is throwing a one-hitter, and we're on the verge of blowing another game. I look up at Trujillo. He's getting steamed again – hands folded across his chest, furrowed brow, big frown. Satch walks over to Dihigo on third base and says, loud enough for everybody in the stands (including Trujillo) to hear him, "I hope your fans brought their winter coats, because it's gonna be a cold day in hell before you touch home plate, my man." And then he slow-walks back to the mound and mows down Showboat Sanchez and Cookie Valdez on 6 fastballs. Then he gets Choo-Choo Diaz to hit a comebacker, which Satch lobs underhand to Payday Thompson and that's that.

Our turn. A zero to zero tie, bottom of the ninth. "How 'bout a run, boys? The needle on Master

Paige's gas tank is leanin' on 'E'" says Satch. Tiant's going to have to face the heart of our lineup – Cool Papa Bell, Deacon Powell, Flash Fowler and then Josh in the cleanup spot.

Cool Papa works the count to 3 and 2, and then drops a perfect bunt up the third baseline. By the time their catcher Pancho Lopez fields the ball, Cool Papa is standing on first base. He's still there after Deacon Powell lines out to second base and Flash Fowler strikes out swinging at the same slow curve he's been whiffing at all day.

So now Josh steps into the box. Josh is angry. Tiant has already plunked him twice – once in the shoulder with a (not that fast) fastball and once in the legs with a wayward emery ball. It's clear he doesn't want anything to do with Josh, because Josh can win the game with one swing, which is what he means to do right now.

Josh steps in – rear foot, front foot, push up that sleeve, eyes burning a hole in Tiant's forehead. Tiant winds and fires – a fastball right at his head. Josh leans back and lets it pass as Cool Papa takes off for second, swiping it easily. Ball one, fastest man in baseball now in scoring position. A shower of boos and jeers rains down from the fans as Josh steps in again. Tiant winds and fires – screwball that starts heading right for Josh, then bends over the inside part of the plate. Strike one. "He's either going to walk him or hit him," says Deacon Powell. "He can't let him get a cut." Josh stands in. Tiant throws a fastball that hits him on the upper thigh. The crowd boos as the umpire whips off his mask with one hand, points at first with the other and barks, "Take your base." Only Josh doesn't move. The umpire moves in front of him and tries it again. "TAKE...YOUR...BASE."

"No. I want my cuts," says Josh. Now Cool Papa calls time and runs in from second base.

"Josh, take your..." but before he can finish, Josh speaks up.

"Third time this clown has hit me. Just 'cuz I been hit don't mean I absolutely have to take first base. I can turn it down and keep hittin' if I want. That's the rule." Is it? Never seen this happen on a ballfield before. Now the Sugar Kings manager Big Cholly Herrera chugs out and both managers make the umpire the meat part of a jawbone sandwich. This goes on for a while until a smiling Dr. Aybar joins the ruckus.

"Excuse me," says the Doc, "perhaps I can help settle this dispute. Ramon," he says to the Umpire, "have you ever encountered a situation of this type before?"

"Never, Doctor Aybar," says the Umpire.

"Can you be certain that what Señor Gibson said – that he has the option of refusing the gift of first base, and may continue batting – is untrue?"

"I cannot," says the Umpire. "However..." But Aybar cuts him off.

"We are in the presence of a man – beloved by his people, admired by the world – who is the soul of wisdom and justice. Perhaps we should ask this man how he would rule on such a matter?" Aybar turns his head and looks at Trujillo, who smiles and nods at Josh. The Umpire turns and bows at Trujillo. "Will that suit you two gentlemen?" he says to the managers. Cool Papa nods, but Cholly starts to argue. Cool Papa pokes him in the chest and motions toward the rifle-toting Guardia Nacional soldiers, now on the top steps of our dugout. Herrera gulps, turns to the umpire and nods.

Now all eyes turn to the Exalted Benefactor. "Mis seres queridos," he bellows, "Traje a estos gran jugadores a nuestro maravilloso país, la joya del Caribe, para que compartan sus dones como beisbolistas. ¡El mañoso intento del Señor Tiant de privar al Señor Gibson la oportunidad de ganar este partido es nada menos que un ESCANDALO!"

"What did he say?" I ask Deacon Powell, who is chortling to himself.

"He's outraged the great players he personally brought here – including yours truly, of course – aren't being allowed to share our magnificent gifts with his beloved potential voters."

"Los Fanaticos Locos" scream their approval, and Trujillo opens his arms to them, swiveling so that he can embrace all 40,000 of them. "Por esa razón," he continues, "He decidido que el Señor Gibson se le permita seguir bateando, como así lo solicito. ¡PLEY BOL!"

"So they're gonna let Josh stay up there?"

"So says El Presidente," says the Deacon. "Play ball!"

I can see the fear in Tiant's eyes as he puts his foot on the pitching rubber. His moon face glistens with sweat as Josh steps back in the batter's box. Tiant is rattled – his next pitch is a slow curve that bounces two feet in front of home plate. The count is three balls and one strike. Tiant steals a quick glance at Trujillo, who is back to glowering. Doesn't look like a walk is going to make the Great Protector of the Dominican Citizenry any happier than plunking Josh with a pitch. Tiant's got to come across with a strike – he knows it, the fans know it, and Josh knows it.

The Sugar King outfielders take a couple of steps back toward the outfield fence. Tiant toes the rubber. Josh steps in. The pitch is another big, slow curve a foot off the plate, but Josh jumps at it and crushes it. Cookie Valdez, the man who robbed Josh in game one, takes three steps toward the wall but there's nothing he can do as the mammoth shot clears the fence by a hundred feet. Cool Papa steps on home and then joins me so we can both shake Josh's hand. As Josh rounds third base, we all get caught in a sudden rain shower – only it ain't rainin' raindrops, it's rainin' gold and silver coins.

I turn and look at the stands. "Los Fanaticos Locos" are on their feet, screaming themselves hoarse, jumping up and down, dancing with each other, waving their Dominican flags, and tossing fistfuls of coins at Josh. After he jumps with both feet on home plate, he walks directly up to Trujillo's box. A smiling Trujillo salutes him, and Josh salutes back. Then Josh motions to our dugout – he wants all the guys to come out and join him. In a flash all the Dragones are part of the scene, holding their caps out to catch the precious metal rainfall. I fill my cap and then my pockets. Every single coin has Trujillo's face on it. Figures.

It's a glorious scene, and it sets the table for game three. We finally get the "laugher" we thought we'd get in game one. Our guys get 8 runs in the first inning, including home runs by Josh and Payday Thompson. Satchel takes himself out after the third inning to rest his arm, and "Bullet" Hampton takes over, mowin' down the Sugar Kings inning after inning. Final score – Dragones 14, Sugar Kings 2. Josh hits another dinger in the 7th. Dragones lead the series 2 games to 1. One more win and we're on our way home. Piece of cake.

We're heroes. Trujillo is all smiles. And now we've won the right to party, and that's just what we're going to do.

CHAPTER TWENTY

The "Club Mojito" was what they call a "drinks club" around these parts, even though it has a band. The "Club Zombie," where we are now, is a "dance club" – the biggest one in Ciudad Trujillo, with a huge dance floor and a big revolving stage like the Crawford Grille, so one merengue band can start up just as the last band is fading out. The revolving stage has the trumpets, saxes and clarinets. The drummers and conga players – I count 12 – are located in nooks and crannies all over the club, and they go non-stop. It's a wild scene. The only grim note is Señor Borgatti and his men. They stand in the shadows and watch the fun.

Like the "Mojito," the "Zombie" has huge painted pictures of the players, only here the pictures show our guys bein' chummy with Trujillo. Bats, balls and gloves decorate the walls. I'm sitting with our guys at the best spot in the place, a huge round table in front of the bandstand. For the first time since we got here, Josh is happy. That's probably because he showed Trujillo and Aybar and "Los Fanaticos Locos" what he could do. Satch is sitting with his girlfriend, the Dominican "Merengue Queen" Nova Quezada, who is dressed in a super flashy red and blue outfit that's nothing but frills, spangles, tassels, flying fringe and puffy sleeves. She's enough covered up to keep from being arrested, but that's about it. Suddenly a dozen waiters descend on the table with big bowls of soup.

"So what we got here?" asks Satchel, bringing a spoon to his lips.

"Mondongo Soup," says the waiter, smiling with pride.

"Looks like something the devil coughed up," says Cool Papa Bell.

"Uh huh," says Satch, mouth full. "And what's in it?"

"Tripe," says the waiter, and Satch immediately coughs what's in his mouth back into the bowl

"Tripe? You mean, like, cow stomach?" he says as the rest of the guys put down their spoons. Dr. Aybar has just about finished his bowl. He smiles and explains.

"Mondongo soup is a beloved national dish here in our homeland. It is indeed the stomach of the cow, soaked in a paste of bicarbonate of soda, and then cooked in hoof jelly for extra flavor. Delicious. Savor it, Señor Paige."

"That's okay, Doc, I'll wait for what's next." Even before he's finished speaking, the next course arrives – giant platters of sizzling meat, with onions and peppers mixed in. "Ah," says Satch, "This is more like it." He grabs the platter from the waiter, pushes a mess of meat onto his plate and starts shoveling it into his mouth.

"Very good, Señor Paige. I see you are an adventurous diner. I hope your teammates share your enthusiasm." Everyone at the table knows that Satch is famous for his nervous stomach, so we're all smiling as Satch looks at Aybar as he swallows that first bite.

"Adventurous? What's adventurous about wolfin' down some hot beef?"

"That's not beef, Satchel. It's better than beef," says Aybar.

"What's better than beef?" asks Satch warily.

"Iguana," And with that Satch spits what's in his mouth into his napkin, bumps his chair over backwards and bolts to the bathroom. We all bust out laughing. He comes back a moment later kinda bug-eyed and hunched over, followed by a waiter with a tray of rum drinks. Dr. Aybar grabs one and holds it up as the waiter hands out the others.

"Gentlemen!" says Aybar. "El Presidente is very pleased with your performance these last two games."

"We kicked their Cuban butts," says Satchel. Aybar smiles and continues.

"The next game is the day after tomorrow. I have guaranteed the Exalted Benefactor of our Homeland that it will be the final victory. Am I safe in making this assumption?" Satch picks up his glass and hoists to the ceiling.

"Victory!" he shouts. All the players pick up their glasses and raise them toward Satch.

"Victory!" yell the players in unison. All the people at tables surrounding us pick up their glasses and raise them toward us.

"VICTORY!" screams the crowd around us. This cheer is so loud the dancers stop dancing, the band stops playing, and everyone in the club joins in.

"VICTORY!!!" Everyone cheers and applauds, and Satch takes a series of deep theatrical bows in all directions. The band plays a raucous fanfare, and the bandleader, a lean bronze sharpy who shines like a light bulb in his white satin cutaway tuxedo, turns to our table.

"Señores and señoritas," he says, "We here at the Club Zombie are very, very honored to have as our guests the greatest baseball players in the world...the pride of the Dominican...our very own Ciudad Trujillo Dragones!" All the guys stand up and join Satchel in taking exaggerated bows as the crowd goes wild. Even Josh joins in, and when he tries to sit back down Satch grabs his jacket and hauls him back up. "In honor of our distinguished guests," continues the bandleader, "the boys and I have learned an Americano 'hot swing' tune by Señor Duke Ellington. We are hoping that the Dragones will show us what they call, in America, 'the jitterbug dance.'" Huge applause as Nova grabs Satchel's arm and drags him out on the dance floor. "In fact, let this be a contest! Everyone here will vote on who is the best jitterbugger! Everyone grab a partner!" Female dancers swarm the table and drag just about every one of the guys onto the floor – only Josh is left. And Julissa walks up to Josh and extends her hand. Where'd she come from?

"Hello, Josh," she says. His eyes light up when he sees her. He stands up and takes her hand, and then looks around nervously. "Borgatti?" she asks. He nods. "Don't worry. Señor Trujillo has ordered him to stay away from us. You and your teammates are heroes. This is a celebration. Come, dance with me."

As soon as Josh and Julissa hit the floor, the band blasts into wild, conga-driven version of "It Don't Mean a Thing If It Ain't Got That Swing." All the guys dance pretty good, but about halfway through the number the floor clears as three couples get serious about grabbing first prize. Payday Thompson works the crowd, taking bets on which couple's gonna win.

Each finalist dances like he plays baseball. Cool Papa Bell is a dervish – he and his partner do twice as many moves as the other couples, including full 360 degree flips, spins, tuck turns, boogie strolls and shim sham shimmys. Satchel, on the other hand, seems to do half as many moves as the others, but each flick of the wrist on those spaghetti arms sends his partner exactly where he wants her – he's like a puppeteer dancing a marionette, only this marionette is as flashy as a neon movie marquee. And Josh – he and Julissa are working up a sweat. They aren't the most graceful couple, but they are the most joyous. The dance floor shakes every time Josh and Julissa jump, spin or hop. The music builds to a rambunctious climax as each couple finishes up with the flashiest move they've got.

One of the musicians takes a bottle of champagne in each hand, pulls the cork out of each with is teeth, then pours the bubbly into a mammoth, brass, two-handled loving cup. The band leader holds up the hand of each of the three female dance contestants and asks the crowd to cheer for a winner. Everyone's smiling, but there's absolutely no doubt about the victor. "And the winner is..." begins the band leader, but before he can finish, Satchel has his hands on the loving cup.

"Satchel Paige and Miss Red Hot Mama Nova Quezada!" says Satch, dumping the champagne over himself and Nova. The crowd goes wild, and the band kicks into "Take the 'A' Train" as Satch and Nova do an energetic encore.

Back at our table, Payday is doling out cash to the winners, and celebrating his new booty. "Had Satch and Nova even money goin' away. Made fifty bucks for two minutes work. Mighty sweet indeed." Satch is signing autographs for the clubbers, and being his normal swaggering self.

"Fact is," says Satch loudly so everyone can hear, "When Satchel Paige leaves baseball, he's gonna open his own string of dancin' academies, the 'Get Hep With Satchel Jitterbuggery.'" He puts his arm around Nova, who has her own group of gawkers. "She's gonna be a part of it," says Satch. Then he leans over and pokes the chest of a sweaty, laughing Josh. "And YOU, my friend, are gonna be ol' Satch's first client."

Julissa defends her man. "He's a wonderful dancer." Satch snorts.

"The man can hit a baseball a country mile, but he can't dance a lick."

"I thought I was very graceful," he says.

"You looked like an elephant trying to stomp out a campfire," says Satch. Josh laughs at this. I can see a mischievous light in Cool Papa's eyes. He sips his rum drink and decides to stir the pot.

"Satch is right about one thing," he says to Nova. "Josh can hit the ball a country mile. Did you know they call him the black Babe Ruth?"

"No," says Nova, looking wide-eyed at Josh. Everyone in the whole world knows Babe Ruth.

"Lot of people think Ruth should be called the white Josh Gibson," says Cool Papa. "In fact, a lot of people say that *Josh* is the best player ever. So good even Satch can't whiff him." Ooooh, fightin' words! Satch jerks his head. His back goes up like an angry cat.

"Ain't no days like that, Papa. Nothing wrong with Josh – hell, he is the best, no doubt – but the player ain't *alive* that Satch can't whiff." Josh usually defers to Satch, gives him the limelight, but this time he scoffs. His pride is hurt, but Satch won't let it alone. "Ol' Satch whiffed them white boys in Alabama. He's whiffin' these Cubans here in the Trujillo-Ville. And Satch could fall outta bed at three o'clock in the morning and whiff Josh Gibson without breakin' a sweat."

"If your mouth was pitching instead of your arm, I'd be worried," says Josh.

"Well, you better be worried, my man, 'cuz someday we're gonna meet up and Satch is gonna blow you down. HUMBLE your sorry ass." The conversation has turned dead serious. The players are quiet. Even Cool Papa, who started the whole thing looks worried.

"I don't think so," says Josh quietly.

"I don't think so either," says Satch. "I KNOW so."

"Don't let your mouth make a promise your arm can't keep."

"You want to shut my mouth? You want to find out who can beat who?" says Satch. "Finish what we started back in Alabama before the Klan got involved?

"Yeah, I do," says Josh. "When and where?"

"Right here. Right now," says Satchel.

"Sounds good," says Josh. He turns to me. "We need us some gear." He nods at the wall behind me.

What the heck, the club's not gonna miss it. The fellas get up and follow Satch and Josh out the door.

Everyone's gathered in the funky alley between the Club Zombie and a beat-up boarding house. Between the full moon and the glare of the Club Zombie's red and blue neon sign, there's just enough light to see what's going on. I take Josh's coat and hand him his bat as Cool Papa Bell paces off the sixty feet, six inches from home plate to the pitcher's mound. Payday Thompson is taking bets from the guys – everyone wants a piece of this action. "Satch? What's your pleasure?" Satch is folding his suit coat and handing it to Nova as he thinks it over.

"Put me down for a Franklin," says Satch. Gulp. A hundred dollars!

"Sounds good to me," says Josh.

"Same rules as before," says Cool Papa Bell, who is gettin' fixed up as the catcher. "One at bat. Satch whiffs Josh, he wins. Josh hits anything in fair territory – as defined by me – Josh wins. I call balls and strikes." This time the pitching rubber is one of the red cloth napkins from our table, and home plate is the platter that brought the sizzling iguana. "We about ready?" says Cool Papa.

"I got a question for Josh," says Satch as he toes the rubber and whirlwinds his arm to loosen it up.

"Just throw the damn ball, Satchel," says Josh, but everyone knows that Satch is gonna have his say no matter what.

"Are you, or are you not the best hitter in all of baseball?"

"That's what they say," says Josh.

"I'm not interested in what THEY say. I'm interested in what YOU say," says Satch.

"You gonna pitch or talk?" asks Josh, but Satch has a point. I've heard everyone else sing Josh's praises, but I've never heard Josh brag on himself.

"All I'm sayin'," says Satch, "Is that if...no, I'm sorry, WHEN Ol' Satch blows your sorry ass away, that will settle ONCE AND FOR ALL TIME who is the best. Not just the best, but the *best of the best.*"

"C'mon, Satch," says Josh, trying hard not to take the bait. Satch turns to his teammates.

"Gentlemen? Am I right? Don't you want to hear the words? We all know we are in the presence of the greatest hitter of our time. The 'black Babe Ruth.' The 'sepia sultan of swat.' Let us hear the man himself acknowledge his greatness." All eyes on Josh. Satch loves to raise the stakes in whatever game he's playing.

"Throw the ball, Satch," says Josh.

"Not until you give us your considered opinion of your own place in the world of organized baseball," says Satch. "*Say...the...words.*" Josh stares at Satch.

"Whoever wins this little fracas, he's the best," says Josh. "You're the best there is, I'll give you that. That said, I've never seen you throw a pitch that I couldn't smoke. That good enough for you?"

"Good enough, my man. And Peanut here is gonna live longer than any of us. He's my witness for posterity. Peanut, when we all get back to the states, put whatever happens here in that newspaper of yours. Agreed?"

"You got it, Satch."

"Now," says Satch, " let's play us some midnight alleyway cham-PEEN-ship baseball."

So here we are – about as far away from the normal way of things as can possibly be. Instead of sunshine, we're playing in the dead of night. Instead of the lush grass of Greenlee Field, we're playin' on cobblestones in a dank alleyway in Ciudad Trujillo. Instead of uniforms, the guys are wearing slacks, dress shirts, suspenders and dress shoes. Instead of the cheers of thousands of fans, all we can hear is the steady jump rhythm of merengue from the club and the occasional produce truck clattering by. None of that makes a bit of difference. This is what baseball is all about – the reason the game was invented. It's a kind of war. Pitcher versus hitter. Unstoppable force versus immovable object. One's gonna win; one's gonna lose.

Josh steps in – back foot, front foot, push up the sleeve, stare at Satch. Satch takes a triple windmill windup and zips a heater high and inside, brushing Josh back off the serving platter. "Ball one," says Cool Papa. Josh steps back in, Satch double-windmills and sizzles one down and away. Josh follows it into Cool Papa's glove. "Ball two," says Cool Papa. Satch is outraged.

"Oh, man! That was a strike, and you know it," he yells at Cool Papa. Cool Papa takes off his mask and walks halfway to the makeshift mound.

"Satchel, save that line of jive for the greenhorn umps in those scruffy towns in Georgia. Josh here has the best batting eye in baseball, and I know every move you're going to make before you make it. I've seen every switch on every pitch you've got in that arm. You're the one who wanted this scrap, and now you've got it. You keep telling everyone how you're going to mow him down. Well, to do that you're gonna have to throw strikes. You'll get a fair shake from me – no slack, but a fair shake. You know where home plate is, and so do I. I don't call 'em as I see 'em, I call 'em as they are. You good with all that?" Satch nods his head. "All right, then." Cool Papa lobs the ball back to him.

Two balls, no strikes. Satch windmills once and slings the 'bullet train' in on Josh's hands. Josh swings and nicks a piece of it off the bat handle. It hits Cool Papa in his mask, which knocks him backwards into some metal garbage cans. Everyone chuckles at this, including Cool Papa, then it's back to business. Two balls, one strike. The next pitch is Satch's infamous "bat dodger," his big, slow hook that just nicks the outside of the platter. "Steee-rike two!" yells Cool Papa. Josh looks back at him. "You heard what I told Satch. Same goes for you, Josh. Play ball."

'Course for Satch to get the most mileage out of this tale when he re-tells it in the future, he's gonna have to blow down Josh on a 3-2 pitch, so it's no surprise when he winds up and hums it neck high and inside for ball three. So this is it, and everyone knows it. One pitch that will decide who is the best of the best. "LAST CHANCE!" yells Payday, and there's a flurry of greenbacks coming his way.

Satch windmills once...then twice...then a third time. He rears back...and vanishes in a blaze of white light. Car horns blare. Brakes squeal and tires bark. What happened to Satch? Did he get hit by a car? I can't see him, or much of anything – headlights in my eyes. What I *can* see is a bunch of silhouettes – guys holding tommy guns, and they're coming toward us. What's going on? They got the Klan out here in the DR? The gangsters get bigger and bigger until they're right on top of us. Two of 'em – Dominicans, I think – have Cool Papa Bell, and three more surround Josh. Nobody says a word. Josh has his bat, and he means to use it. Finally the biggest one says, "We are not here to harm you, but you must come with us."

"What's this about?" asks Josh.

"Just come with us. You will find out soon enough." If he wanted to kill us, I figure he would have done it by now.

"Wherever you're takin' us, the boy comes too or I don't go. I'm takin' care of him," says Josh. The Dominicans look at each other and nod. And then they march us back to the cars, blindfold us and bind our hands with rope. And it's funny. The last thing I see before they tie on the blindfold is a shadowy figure across the street. Maximo Borgatti, arms folded, watching this whole thing, and smiling.

CHAPTER TWENTY-ONE

"Gentlemen, welcome!" Somebody yanks the blindfold off, and I blink into a burst of white light. My eyes adjust, and I can see that we all – Josh, Cool Papa, Satchel, Payday and yours truly – are looking into the face of a smiling Tyler Underwood, dressed in his usual pineapple-and-hula-girl-Hawaiian shirt, white slacks and black and white spectator shoes. A couple of bodyguards – one broad and beefy, the other tall and wiry – untie our wrists and ankles. Wherever this is, it's the second nicest place we've been since we got here, besides the Presidential Palace. Some kind of luxury hotel suite is my guess – big spacious rooms, cream-colored walls, overstuffed chairs and sofas, and a humungous table full of food. More burly Dominican bodyguards with holstered pistols guard the door. "I apologize for the rough methods that were used to bring you here. I have my reasons. I couldn't really approach you at the ballpark or the hotel. I saw my chance there in the alley, and I took it."

"Man, I have HAD IT with this jive!" says Satchel, pacing up and down as he rubs his wrists to work out the rope burns. "We came down here to play a little baseball. It's our business, you know? Like you're in the sugar business, is my guess. That's all we want to do, play baseball. Instead we been getting' shot at, kidnapped, roughed up, beaten down…"

"Satchel…" says Underwood, but Satch isn't done yet.

"I feel like I been dropped into the lion cage at the circus. No matter where we turn, we get hammered by somebody wants us taken down a peg, and this time that'd be YOU."

"If you'll just listen to what I have to say…' says Underwood, but Satch still isn't finished.

"I figure it's about time *somebody* told us what's goin' on around here. What's the story, morning glory? Tell Satchel what he's gotten his bad self into. He done stuck his foot in a bear trap, that's clear enough. But what *kind* of trap? Is the trap gonna take his leg off, or kill him entirely? Tell me, my man. I gots to know. Tell Satchel if his future has passed, or if he's gonna live to pitch another day."

"Okay," says Underwood. "Fair enough. As I'm sure you've figured out by now, I know something about you boys." He plops himself down in one of the flowery over-stuffed armchairs and gets serious. "I know you work for a racketeer named Gus Greenlee. Well, imagine a world where Gus Greenlee not only owns the Pittsburgh Crawfords AND the Crawford Grille AND the policy game in Pittsburgh, but he's also the Mayor, the Governor, the President, the Chief of Police and head of the Army. He has the power to take anything else he wants. If it's not nailed down, it's his, and if he can pry it up, it's not nailed down. That's who you're working for. And that's who I'm trying to beat."

"Trujillo," says Satchel.

"Trujillo," says Underwood. He looks at Josh. "You like a nice juicy steak, Josh?"

"Who doesn't?"

"You order a steak here, you pay Trujillo. Trujillo owns the cattle ranches, the slaughterhouses and the cafes. Cigarette after your meal? Trujillo owns the tobacco plantations. And I'm sure you'd like a nice cup of coffee with that meal. Guess who owns the coffee farms? Cream in your coffee? Trujillo grabbed the dairies six months ago, just swooped down and took 'em. He rakes every dollar of profit into his own account, and everyone who works for him has to kick him 10% of their salary."

"Like we did," says Josh.

"Like you did," says Underwood.

"Not me," says Satchel.

"Point taken," says Underwood.

"How 'bout the sugar in that coffee?" asks Josh. Underwood smiles.

"Ahhh. Sugar is the one product Trujillo hasn't been able to grab. At least not yet."

"Why not?" asks Cool Papa.

"My friends, the Dominican Republic is an island made of sugar. It's the biggest crop, the biggest export, and by far the biggest source of cash for the Exalted Benefactor. The people I represent – a confederation of American sugar companies – planted the crops that built these plantations. We built the factories that process the sugar. We own the boats that carry this sugar all over the world. We did all this before El Presidente ever took office. In fact, we – American sugar, the people I work for – put Trujillo in office. We made him a deal. He'd leave us alone if we'd look the other way while he took everything else. Turns out it was a deal with the devil." He snorts at his own joke. "*Nothing* is ever enough for Trujillo. He wants it all. He wants to take everything we've got here in the Dominican, and pay us with a swift kick in the rear end. That's not going to happen."

"That's where we come in, right?" says Cool Papa Bell. Underwood smiles.

"Right. That's why I grabbed you. You're right in the middle of this, and I can help you. I have an offer."

"What kind of offer?" asks Satchel, before Josh can jump in.

"I know Aybar gave you 30 large in a suitcase for the series, and you split it with your pals." I remember Satch telling him that Aybar gave him 50 large. Underwood knew the truth all the time. Now

Underwood looks over his shoulder and motions for the beefy minion. He hands Underwood a leather travel bag that the big man opens in front of us. "50,000 cash American, for two wins. Satchel, you take what you want and make your own deal with Josh and Cool Papa." Everyone stares at the money for a long moment.

"Something I still don't understand, and I hope you'll enlighten me," says Josh.

"If I can," says Underwood.

"Why is winnin' this series worth so damn much money to everybody?" asks Josh. "It's just baseball."

"Just baseball? Maybe back in the States, Josh. But the people down here? They're baseball crazy. It's practically a sickness." Underwood stares at Josh. "I mean, c'mon – have you ever had people throw money at you – cash money – for hitting a home run?"

"No," says Josh. "I guess it is different."

"You think it's a coincidence that Trujillo scheduled the election the day after the series ends, if it goes all five games? Trujillo has got to win this series. GOT to. If Trujillo's team – the Dominican national team that he himself put together – loses the series, he loses face. He loses the election. He loses power. And if that happens, well…."

"Well what?" says Cool Papa. Underwood stares at the guys, and lowers his voice.

"He's a dead man, that's what. Here's what you don't know, gentlemen, and if you're lucky, you'll never know. Trujillo has done something. Something bad. Worse than bad. Evil. Something that boggles the mind." Underwood stops, takes a pack of Lucky Strike cigarettes out of his inside suit pocket, and shakes one out. The skinny bodyguard snaps open a silver Zippo lighter, flicks the flint wheel and lights it. "Where was I?"

"Something that would boggle our minds," says Cool Papa.

"That's right. Something that, if it comes out – which it will, if he loses – will put him right up there with the great villains of history, like Genghis Khan and Vlad the Impaler." This stops everybody cold. *What did he do?*

"We've met this guy, Tyler. He's not some gangster," says Satchel.

"Yeah, Satchel? *You...have...no...idea*," says Underwood. He's dead serious, and he's scaring the pants off us.

"You're sayin' he's killed people?" says Josh.

"That's right."

"How many?"

"Thousands." *Thousands?* I gulp. Everyone stares at Underwood.

"Not personally, of course. Borgatti and the Guardia Nacional, they're the ones with the machetes. Trujillo tells him *who* to kill," says Underwood.

"Okay. Say we take your offer," says Josh. "Not sayin' we will, but say we do. How are you gonna stop Trujillo from..."

"Killing you?"

"Yeah."

"He's got his army. I've got mine. And my Army is the United States Marines. Those sugar plantations are American property, you betcha. You take my offer..." says Underwood, pausing to make sure Satch and Josh are looking right at him, "and here's what'll happen. First, I'll get you and your money out of the country, safe and sound." Now he stares right at Satch. "Next, my people will put together a team – Satchel Paige and His American Sugar Kings. The team you've always wanted."

"What do you mean by that?" asks a wary Satch. This is man that's been lied to by everyone.

"Close your eyes, Satch. In fact, all of you close your eyes." Josh looks at Satch, who shrugs and nods. We close our eyes. "You're back in the States, in your magnificent new uniforms, designed to your specifications, Satchel. You're not on some crummy sandlot, you're in a major league stadium. Forbes Field, Yankee Stadium, Sportsman's Park in St. Louis. Satchel is on the mound, Josh is behind the plate, Cool Papa is in center field. Satchel winds up and delivers. Joe DiMaggio swings and misses, and 50,000 fans go completely wild." Underwood lets us finish that word-picture in our minds. Then we open our eyes and look at him.

“Pretty picture,” says Satch. “But what’s the deal?”

“You and your hand-picked teammates play in big cities, in the best ballparks. A 2 year schedule of dates, with an option for 2 more, at twice the dough that Greenlee pays you.”

“Guaranteed,” says Satch.

“Guaranteed,” says Underwood, “and paid up front by certified check.”

“And these big league stadiums, they let us use their locker rooms?” asks Cool Papa. I’m sure he remembers playing at Forbes Field in Pittsburgh and having to get dressed on the bus. Tyler laughs.

“For what I’m gonna pay ‘em, they damn well better let you use the locker rooms,” laughs Underwood.

“No rickety busses,” says Josh.

“Trains only.”

“My own Pullman car,” says Satchel.

“Done.”

“And none o’ them scabby boarding houses with roaches the size of house cats,” says Satchel.

“The best hotels I can book, with clean sheets on every bed and a shower in every room,” says Underwood. “It’s a great deal, boys. Maybe the best you’ll ever get. Hell, after those major league owners see you playing in their ballparks and traveling on their trains and staying in their hotels and beating their best players in front of sell-out crowds, how can they keep you out of the big leagues?”

"Just one more question," says Josh.

"Go ahead," says Underwood.

"You'll be paying the three of us to jump to the Sugar Kings. What about the rest of the guys?"

"Rest of the guys?" says Underwood, baffled.

"The rest of the Crawfords. The ones who will still be with Trujillo if we join the Sugar Kings." Underwood furrows his brow. He takes a last puff on his smoke, and snuffs it in big crystal ashtray.

"They're…uhhh….they're not part of this deal, Josh."

"So what you're sayin' is, they're on their own." Underwood's look lets us know that's so. Josh looks at Satchel, who won't meet his eyes. They both know what Trujillo will do to those guys if they lose. And this time the firing squad won't lower their rifles.

"Here's the best I can do," says Underwood. "After you boys win that last game, I'll have my security men grab the others, take the team to the airport, and see that you get out of here safely," says Underwood. He makes it sound like a cakewalk.

"Trujillo has a lot of soldiers. It's his country. What makes you think you'll get to our guys first?" says Josh.

"Look, Josh," says Underwood. "Those boys knew what they were getting into when they…."

"That ain't true!" yells Josh, as he vaults up and starts and pacing. "*None* of us had *any idea* of what we were getting into." He walks over to Underwood and leans down into his face. "You honestly think we'd have come down here for any amount of money if we knew we were gonna get *shot* if we lost? *Shot? For playing ball?* That's crazy!"

"Now let's hold on," says Satchel. "We're this close to makin' the deal that Satchel's dreamed of his entire damn life." He turns to Underwood. "Tyler, can you guarantee that we – and by we, I mean the whole bunch of us, including the fellas that play for Trujillo – that we will get outta this place in one piece?" Tyler rubs his chin as he thinks about this.

"I could lie to you boys and nod my head. But the truth is, I'm not sure. I *can absolutely guarantee* the safety of you three, and the boy here, if you come over to the Sugar Kings. And I *guarantee* I'll put everybody from my personal security force and every Marine the local base will give me on that field. And yes, I think that'll be enough. But like I said, if Trujillo loses, he loses everything. He might panic. And if that happens, even you fellas....well..."

"That's an honest answer, Mr. Underwood. I appreciate it," says Josh. "That's why we can't..." Satch cuts him off.

"We need to talk about this 'mongst ourselves," says Satch. He looks at Underwood. "BY ourselves. If you don't mind."

"Be my guest," says Underwood. "Take all the time you need, as long as you tell me right away and your answer is 'yes.'" He chuckles, lifts himself up and walks out of the room with the two bodyguards right behind.

I got a pretty good idea what's going to happen now. Satchel versus Joshua, with Cool Papa in the middle. Like always.

"I been playin' ball for 'bout nine years, and I ain't never heard nobody offer no black man what he's offering us," says Satchel. "And this ain't hot air, neither. This is a bunch of millionaires that need us so they can stay in business down here. Hell, what we're doin' for them, we're a damn bargain no matter what they pay us."

"Ain't no doubt about that," says Cool Papa.

"So I say we take the damn money," he says to Cool Papa. Then he turns to Josh. "Long daddy green is talkin' to you, Josh," says Satchel. "He's sayin' it's about time you make what you're worth."

"Ain't about money, Satch," says Josh. "It's about doin' what's right. Those other guys are depending on us."

"What's RIGHT," says Satch, raising his voice, "is that we do what's RIGHT for us. You heard him say he'll get the other guys out..."

"No, that's NOT what I heard him say, Satchel. None of us heard that!" Josh thunders. He's got our full attention. "What I heard was a white man beating his gums about 'doin' his best' to rescue the guys. Only if Trujillo loses, who knows what's going to happen? His promise and ten cents'll buy you a cup of coffee at the local beanery."

"Look," says Satch. "We're in a mess o' trouble, ain't no doubt about that. Fact is, nobody here including Peanut knows what's gonna happen. We could stay with Trujillo, lose two games and get shot. We could stay with Trujillo, win the next game and get shot."

"Unlikely," says Cool Papa Bell.

"Agreed. But possible. Everybody keeps tellin' us this guy is crazy."

"We could stick with Trujillo, win this last game and get out of here alive," says Josh. "That's most likely."

"Why?" says Satch, heat in his voice. "'Cuz he promised? We're his pets. We're his 'Dominican national team.' The people here love us. What's in it for him to let us go?" Josh has no answer for this. "Here's something else that could happen. We could jump to the Sugar Kings and win the last two games. Hell, if this guy really has the U.S. Marines on his side, he can keep Borgatti's boys from shooting down a bunch of ballplayers in front of 40,000 people. And then we're on easy street. Think of it, fellas. Pullman cars, big league ballparks, first class hotels, and our best shot at the big leagues. That's good enough for ol' Satchel, yessiree."

"You trust Underwood?" asks Josh.

"Hell no. But at least he ain't crazy like Trujillo," says Satch.

"So," says Cool Papa, "I guess it comes down to which one is the least likely to get us shot."

"Yeah, sounds 'bout right. So what'll we do?" asks Josh.

"We vote," says Satch. He turns to me. "Sorry, Peanut, but it's just gonna be the three of us."

"What?" He can't do this to me!

"Why's that?" asks Josh.

"He's just a kid," says Satch.

"Am NOT!"

"The way these guys figure it, he's one of us, " says Josh. "He's just as likely to get shot as any of us."

"Yeah!"

"That ain't true," says Satch. "What do you think, Papa?" Cool Papa looks at me, then back at Satchel.

"Well, let's see," says Papa. "When Trujillo threw us that party at the prison with the firing squad, he lined Peanut up with the rest of us. Guess that means he gets a full vote."

"That makes four votes. So what happens if this ends up a two-two tie?" asks Satch.

"Let's ask Peanut," says Josh. He turns to me. "What do we do then?"

"In that case," I say, "I guess we keep talkin' until somebody changes his vote."

"Hells bells, that could take *days*!" says Satch.

"Yeah, well, we're talkin' 'bout our *lives* here. What's a day or two if we live to tell the tale?" says Josh. "Everybody gets a vote, keep talkin' till we break the tie. Done."

"Sounds good to me," says Cool Papa. "Anybody want to say something before we vote?"

"Yeah," says Satchel. "End of the day, this is about the money. The people that pay us the most have the biggest investment in us getting' out of here alive. We be fools if we don't take it when we've got the chance, because we may never get another chance like this as long as we live. Ain't that right, Peanut?" Everybody looks at me, including Josh.

"Yeah, Peanut. Is that what this is about? Money?" Josh is staring at me."Underwood's gonna pay us $50,000, Peanut. That's a lot of sugar. Know how much you're in for?" Satch is smiling as he moves in on me.

"How much?"

"Try FIVE...THOUSAND...DOLLARS. Five large, cash," says Satchel. "You can buy your mama the swankiest house on the Hill with that kind of cabbage."

I look away from Satch and see Josh. He's still staring at me. I think of what he said about money, and about doin' the right thing.

I turn back to Satch. "Ain't just about the money, Satch." Satch's face falls. He thought my vote was in the bag. "Money's a part of it, sure, but...well, when I joined the Crawfords, I joined a *team*. Team sticks together, even when you hit a rough patch."

"*Especially* when you hit a rough patch," says Josh.

Nobody says a thing, but there's a whole lot of staring going on – Satch at me, Josh and Cool Papa at Satch, Me at the floor.

"So," says Cool Papa, breaking the hush, "We ready to take that vote?"

"Yeah," says Josh. "Everybody in favor of jumping to the Sugar Kings, raise your hand." Satch's hand shoots up. He looks at Cool Papa, who looks away. Then Satchel's eyes drill into mine.

"Put up your hand, Peanut," says Satch. "This is your big chance. Think of your mama. Think about handing her five thousand smackers. Take you and her ten years to make that much dough. And there's more where that came from."

"More?" I ask.

"There's the money you're gonna make as my *personal assistant* on your two-year tour with the Satchel Paige All-Stars." Satch stares off, spinning a dream for the two of us. "Pullman cars, comfy beds in nice hotels, big chocolate sodas in fancy restaurants…" I think about this. Man, would I like that! Heaven on earth! Then I look at Josh. He doesn't say a thing, just looks back at me with his serious face. I think about what he told me – about what happened to him when he was 19. About what happens when you do what you want instead of doing what's right.

I swallow hard. Forgive me, Mama. "Can't do it, Satchel," I say in a voice barely above a whisper. "It just ain't right. The other guys…"

"FORGET them other guys! They ain't here! They ain't got a vote. You wanna live a happy life, you gotta go out and grab what's best for YOU!" he shouts at me. I turn to Josh for help, and I see the other guys on the team standing behind him, like shadows. Good ol' Deacon Powell is smilin' at me, and suddenly I know exactly what I have to do.

"Those other guys – Payday, Deacon, Willie, the whole bunch – they're depending on us, Satch. What if they were here, and our lives were in their hands? Hell, you think the Deacon would hesitate a second? He'd know just what to do. And that's what we have to do."

"Good boy, Peanut," says Cool Papa. Josh smiles and gives me a single nod. I've just lost $5,000, but I feel like a million. I know I've done the right thing. Feels good.

"Everyone in favor of stickin' with the current arrangement, raise your hand," says Josh. He raises his hand. Cool Papa looks at Satchel, then raises his hand. Satchel looks at me, his last hope. Decision time. "Forgive me, Mama," I say to myself as I raise my hand up. Three to one. Satchel slams his hand down on the table.

"Buncha damn FOOLS," he says, fuming.

"Maybe," says Josh. "But it's what we decided. And we need to know that you'll keep your word."

"Don't worry 'bout me," says Satchel. "Just worry about winnin' this last game."

CHAPTER TWENTY-TWO

October 14, 1937

Everybody's in uniform and ready to run out onto the field as a smiling Dr. Enrique Aybar enters the dressing room with Julissa Perez at his side. "Gentlemen, a word."

"Go head, Doc," says Cool Papa.

"Today is a glorious day. Today is the day when the hopes and dreams of the Dominican people will be realized. Today is the day when your magnificent victory will ensure that our Exalted Benefactor will continue to bring prosperity and abundance to this wondrous land."

"It's just us winnin' a damn ballgame," says Satch. He's sulking in front of his locker. Never seen him so crabby before a game.

"Yes, quite so," says Aybar. "I just wanted you to understand what will happen immediately after your victory."

"Trujillo's gonna throw us some big wingding, right?" says Josh. Dr. Aybar smiles and adjusts the red carnation in the lapel of his immaculate ice cream suit.

"Yes, but before that. Miss Julissa Perez has arranged things so her movie cameras can capture this moment in its fullness. Julissa?" A smiling Julissa steps forward, as full of sparkle as a carnival barker.

"After Señor Paige retires the last Sugar Kings batter, you will not return to your dugout. You will remain on the field, clustered around the pitcher's mound as a thousand white doves of victory are released, and Dr. Trujillo is carried onto the field by the Elite Honor Corps of the Guardia Nacional."

"Did you say, 'a thousand white doves?'" asks Cool Papa, amazed.

"That's right, they'll be released right in front of two of my cameras. And then El Presidente's 115-piece ceremonial band will line the base paths and play an original composition, entitled 'God in the Sky, Trujillo On the Earth, All Blessings to the Enlightened Steward of our Shared National Destiny.'" Deacon Powell leans down and whispers in my ear.

"Whew! The melody of *that* tune has some heavy lifting to do."

"I keep waitin' to hear the words 'party, dancing, food, and women' but I ain't heard those words yet," says Satch, staring at Aybar. The guys chuckle, but Aybar is in such a good mood he doesn't take the bait. He just nods at Julissa, who keeps talkin'.

"After this song comes the awarding of the Trujillo Trophy." Aybar snaps his fingers, and two "Guardia Nacionals" roll in a gigantic mystery object on a four-wheeled dolly, covered by a tarp. Julissa says "Señor Gibson, Señor Bell, and Señor Paige will join El Presidente at home plate in front of a bank of five cameras as the trophy is revealed." She looks at Aybar, who yanks off the tarp to reveal the "Trujillo Trophy," which is – you guessed it – a gold-plated, life-sized statue of Dr. Rafael Trujillo, smiling, with one hand raised in greeting and the other leaning on a baseball bat, which looks really odd since Trujillo is dressed in his army uniform, not baseball gear.

"Wow. That is really something," says Cool Papa, staring at the statue. I don't think he means this like Aybar thinks he means it.

"This will be a big moment. We need you to show us how you feel," says Julissa.

"How do you mean?" asks Josh.

"This is the climax of our drama, Señor Gibson," says Aybar. "Let us see the joy you feel at coming here. Let our people share your gladness. We need one of you to step forward and express your gratitude to Dr. Trujillo for bringing you here to represent his beloved countrymen. Which of you will embrace this honor?" Satch has been rubbing neatsfoot oil into his glove since Aybar started talking, and doesn't look up now. All the guys look at one another, and then at Josh. Interesting moment. When we came here, Satch was definitely the man in charge. Now that's changed.

"I'll thank him," says Josh.

"With *enthusiasm*," says Aybar

"I'll kiss him, if you want."

"Just a handshake is sufficient."

"Excellent," says Julissa.

"And then," says Aybar, "you will urge the fans to acknowledge this victory by endorsing El Presidente at the ballot box, to return him to office, yes? In your own words, of course."

"Sure. I can do that," says Josh. "Vote for El Presidente. Is that it?"

"Almost," says Julissa. "All that remains is for the Dragones players to hoist El Presidente Trujillo on your shoulders and carry him through the gate near the third base side, pausing and smiling as you pass another of my cameras, and then deliver him gently to his waiting limousine."

"Fellas? You good with that?" asks Josh. Everyone nods. Julissa steps back. Aybar looks at Satch.

"And then, Señor Paige, the party. At the palace of El Presidente. Quite unlike any party you have ever attended, I assure you. Imagine the ultimate celebration – this will be better. Food, dancing, and, yes, women. Including, Señor Paige, a certain Miss Nova Quezada. She is quite taken with you." He smiles at Satch, who finally looks over at him. Satch forces a smile that's closer to a grimace. What's wrong with him? Still carrying a grudge from the vote?

"And what happens the morning after the party?" asks Josh.

"The party will last till dawn. At that time, you will be escorted in limousines to the Pan Am Clipper for your return voyage to the United States, with our thanks and good wishes," says Dr. Aybar. "Of course, this is contingent on your victory in today's game." Aybar stares at Satchel, who finally looks him in the eye.

"You can blow up the balloons, bake the cakes, break out the pom-poms and put the bubbly on ice, Doc" says Satchel. "Satchel's had about all he can stand of El Presidente Trujillo's hospitality-at-gunpoint. Ol' Satch may even throw himself a no-hitter, just to make sure that damn Clipper leaves on time."

"Yes," says Aybar, a little uncomfortable with Satch's downbeat attitude. "A no-hitter would be delightful, but a simple, decisive victory will suffice. I will leave you now and deliver the news to El Presidente that the celebration will proceed as planned."

We're in the bottom of the ninth inning, and you can cut the tension here at Rafael Trujillo Park with a sugar cane machete. Satchel's no-hitter lasted two-thirds of an inning, when the Sugar Kings catcher, Pancho Lopez, smashed a hanging curveball over the left field fence. Satchel's been in trouble just about every inning. His fastball is fast but it ain't "Satchel" fast, and he can't seem to get his curveball to snap when it crosses the plate. He's like he was back in game one, only this time he ain't got an excuse 'cuz he ain't been out partyin' all night. He and Josh are barely speakin' to one another, and when they do speak on the bench it's only to insult each other. "We're playin' a real game today, Satch. This ain't battin' practice," says Josh.

"Satchel's getting' 'em out."

"Satchel's doggin' it. You can fool those loonies in the stands, and you might even fool some of these guys, but I'm your damn catcher. You're servin' up fat ones."

"Tain't so," says Satch, but he won't look any of the fellas in the eye, especially Josh.

"Damn well is so."

"You want me to take the rest of the day off?"

"Already doin' that," says Josh. Everyone's staring at the two of them, including me and Cool Papa. "What I WANT…is for you to bring what you *got*. ALL of it. Bear down and get us a win, so we can get outta here in one damn piece."

Lucky for all of us, the fellas playing behind Satch bail him out again and again. Deacon Powell and Willie Tatum turn five double plays. In the sixth inning, Satch walks both Martin Dihigo and Choo-Choo Diaz on three-two counts, which brings Crush Coleman to the plate. Satchel serves him a sidearm fastball, which Coleman pops up to short centerfield. Both runners take off because there ain't no way anybody snags that, except that Cool Papa Bell ain't anybody. Cool Papa runs flat out, leaps for the ball, grabs it, then does a complete forward roll and comes up at a full tilt. He steps on second to double up Dihigo then tags Diaz for the first unassisted triple play I ever seen. Even El President Trujillo is on his feet for this one. Everybody goes wild.

So now it's the bottom of the ninth, two outs, Ciudad Trujillo Dragones up by a single run, 5-4. Cookie Valdez is on third, Alejandro Garcia on second, Pablo Marcel on first – all walked by Satch after he got two quick outs. The marching band is lined up in front of the stands on the first base side. Hundreds of Guardia Nacional soldiers with blue and red uniforms, shiny chrome helmets and automatic rifles are lined up along the third base side. I can see eleven newsreel movie cameras shooting the game – eight trained on the field, three aimed full time on El Presidente Trujillo. He's hamming it up good – smiling, waving at everybody, and bouncing babies on his lap to show what a great guy he is.

Now the most feared power hitter in all of Latin America, Orestes "Showboat" Sanchez is getting ready to dig into the batter's box. Josh calls time and walks out to the mound. I'm up on the top step of the dugout and I can hear every word. Josh is fightin' mad.

"You just have to put on a damn show, don't you?" says Josh, angry.

"What do you..."

"Walkin' those three so you could have Sanchez. Well, you got what you wanted, Satchel."

"I didn't..."

"SHUT UP!" Josh screams loud enough so that everyone in the ballpark can hear him, including Trujillo. "What I want is for you to paint the outside black of the plate with three red-hot buzzers, at the knees."

"That's exactly what ol' Satch intends to do."

"Then you shouldn't have no trouble doin' it, because you got plenty left, what with you doggin' it all day."

"Play ball!" shouts the home plate umpire, but Josh isn't done yet, and neither is Satchel.

"I ain't been doggin' it..."

"Now you listen here, Satchel." Josh turns and looks at Sanchez, a mean-looking fireplug who is waving a big piece of lumber just outside the batter's box. Satch stares at him too. "That bastard is the best high fastball hitter in the world. Even better than me."

"Yeah? So?"

"IN...THE...WORLD," says Josh, getting right up in Satchel's face.

"Satchel Paige didn't get us here by being a chump. You catch, and let ol' Satch strike this guy out."

As Josh walks back behind home plate, I look at the stands – seems like every single fan is makin' a bet with every other fan on how this is gonna turn out. Josh squats down, wigwags a sign, and sets up low and outside as the ump leans over him. Satchel windmills once...then twice...and now a third time, and the moment he lets it go I get a sick feeling in my stomach 'cuz I know just what's going to happen. I see it all, and there's nothin' I can do about it. Satch delivers a lollipop – a big, fat, letter-high fastball right down the pipe. Hell, I could hit this one out of the park with the handle of a toilet plunger. Sanchez swings. CRACK! Cool Papa doesn't even chase it. He just turns and watches it clear the bleachers.

Josh knows what I know even before I know it. As soon as the ball leaves Satchel's hand, Josh gets up out of his crouch. By the time Sanchez has hit the ball, Josh is standing, mask off, staring at Satch. He's not screaming. He's not even talking. He's just staring at him. He continues to stand there as all three runners tag home and then mob Sanchez as he crosses the plate. I walk out next to Josh, but he doesn't look at me, just keeps staring at Satch. Satch won't look back at him. He hunches on the mound trying to look upset, like what happened was some horrible mistake instead of his plan to hand one to the Sugar Kings and then take Underwood's money and to hell with the fellas who came with him.

The Guardia Nacionals surge toward Trujillo to protect him from "Los Fanaticos Locos," but the fans are more interested in mobbing the field. In the midst of this madness, Josh still stands there, hands on hips, looking at Satchel. Finally, Satchel looks back at him. Both are grim, staring statues, standing stock still like lighthouses in the middle of a swirling, crashing wave of crazed fans. I'm looking right at them when one – Satchel – vanishes, swept up in the mob.

A bayonet jabs me in the back. I see another in Josh's back. A couple of Guardia Nacionals have the drop on us, with eight more behind them. Maximo Borgatti breaks through the group and stands in front of Josh. He smiles a smile that makes my blood run cold. It's a smile of pure, gleeful hatred. Borgatti screeches an order at his men so the spittle sprays on Josh's face. Then we're frog-marched toward who knows where. I don't know what holds me upright, my legs are shakin' so bad, but Josh looks cool. If his insides are scared, they aren't talkin' to his face.

CHAPTER TWENTY-THREE

The giant iron doors clang shut behind us after Josh, Cool Papa, and I are thrown on the dirty cobblestone floor. We're in a very nasty part of the worst place on earth – Nigua Prison. The place is filled with rats. As we're marched down here we pass an electric chair, a couple of torture chambers, and a block of cells holding men who look like filthy, hollow-eyed skeletons.

"Do you know what we call those men? Frogs. Our orders are to starve them to death. Can you guess their crime?" the smirking soldier asks as we pass these living corpses.

"I'm sure you're gonna tell us," says Cool Papa.

"They refused to remove their hats when El Presidente passed before them during our Restoration Day parade."

"That's it?" I say. Both Josh and Cool Papa stare at me with a "Shut up!" look.

"He is the sun in our sky. Every loyal Dominican citizen is asked to remove his hat, place it over his heart, and bow. Not so difficult, but some cannot bring themselves to show deference. These men are learning the cost of false pride."

Now we're in this horrible place – a dank, airless stone box. The only furniture is a small table in the center, and two wooden chairs. The rats here must be scared of something, but it sure ain't us. They sniff around us like they can't wait for us to fall asleep so they can ring the dinner bell.

"What's going on?" I ask Josh.

"El President does not lose," says Cool Papa, mournfully echoing the words of Dr. Aybar.

"Are they trying to scare us?" I ask.

"After lining us up in front of a firing squad? How is this gonna scare us anymore than that?" asks Cool Papa.

"Listen here," says Josh. "El Presidente isn't gonna murder his best chance to win these games, and that's us."

"Ah!" says Borgatti, throwing open the iron gates and entering the dungeon with two of his prize goons. "So, Señor Gibson, you believe that El Presidente *needs* you."

"Damn right. To beat the American sugar companies," says Josh. Borgatti chuckles at him.

"I have been with El Presidente since he took power. I helped El Presidente defeat the tobacco growers, the salt mining interests, the cattle barons, the lottery thieves, the newspaper owners – and now the sugar business will be ours. Do you know how we've done this?"

"With a loaded gun," says Josh.

"Precisely. We studied the way you Norteamericanos achieve your goals. A gun to the head. Those who help us, live. Those who fight us, die."

"We're helpin' you," says Josh. "But we can't help you in here."

"Yes," says Borgatti, "El Presidente still believes you can be useful." Hmmm. I notice he uses "El Presidente" in a way that doesn't include Maximo Borgatti. That's bad. "In fact, El Presidente has ordered that you be kept safe for the next game. I, his most trusted assistant, have taken on this assignment personally. And I have decided that the one place you will be safe from the malign influence of Señor Underwood is here, in Nigua Prison."

"I don't feel very safe," says Josh, looking at his blank-eyed, gun-wielding goons.

"What are you afraid of?" asks Borgatti. It's like he's daring Josh to say the words.

"Only one thing I can think of that scares me," says Josh.

"Please, share your fear. Perhaps I can alleviate your alarm, and that of your friends." Josh looks him right in the eye and lays it out.

"I'm afraid that El Presidente Trujillo trusts his loyal servant, Señor Maximo Borgatti. He thinks Señor Borgatti will do what he is told."

"Yes. Very good. He does think that," says Borgatti.

"Only Señor Borgatti has a whole 'nother thing goin' on. He's got his own ideas about what to do."

"And what are those ideas?" asks Borgatti.

"Best I can figure it, Señor Borgatti wants revenge for me kickin' his ass in that nightclub. Stoppin' him from beatin' up on a woman. So he figures to kill me here...."

"Your first misstep, Señor Gibson. You will not die here, unless by accident. But you will die. I will be revenged. Go on."

"So he figures to kill me," says Josh. "Maybe kill all three of us." Including me!

Borgatti nods at this. Josh continues. "So I gotta ask myself, what happens if El Presidente loses the last two games and gets his butt kicked out of the country? What happens to Señor Maximo Borgatti?" Borgatti smiles. He's enjoying this, kind of like a cat likes playing with a mouse before the cat eats it.

"Are you saying that I'm disloyal to the Enlightened Steward of our Shared National Destiny?" says Borgatti.

"Yeah," says Josh. "I think I got it worked out."

"Pray tell," says Borgatti.

"You're the head of the secret police, the SIM, along with the Guardia Nacionals," says Josh. "Even if Trujillo gets the heave-ho, whoever comes in next..."

"Such as the puppet president controlled by the Señor Underwood and the American sugar thieves," says Borgatti.

"They'll need you, because you've got the guns. You can stop a rebellion. Or start one," says Josh. "So, in other words..."

"If the Dragones win, I win. And if the Sugar Kings win..."

"You win," says Josh.

"Very astute," says Borgatti.

"Yeah. Except for one thing."

"And what might that be?" says Borgatti.

"You and Señor Trujillo been up to some mischief. Done something bad." Borgatti's face darkens at this.

"Who told you this?"

"Underwood," says Josh. "Didn't tell us what it was, but it had him spooked."

"He was lying. To win you over," says Borgatti angrily.

"Don't think so," says Josh.

"So what if he wasn't?" says Borgatti. "What difference does it make?"

"The difference is that if the Sugar Kings win, no way Underwood and his pals are going to trust you. They'll get rid of you the first chance they get," says Josh

"Unless I get rid of them. Or make a deal with them," says Borgatti. "And that deal has already been discussed." There's a long pause in the conversation.

Josh is chewing on this. I can see a light bulb go on over his head. He gets it, and "it" ain't good.

"Underwood is gonna let *you* become the new Trujillo. So this is really about you double-crossing your boss and takin' over," says Josh.

"That's one way of putting it," says Borgatti. "I would state it differently."

"Which is how?"

"That I will finally assume my *rightful place* in the government." The last piece of the puzzle clicks in place.

"So killing us..."

"...benefits Maximo Borgatti. It facilitates my inevitable rise to the Presidency. I should have been the maximum leader of this country from the start. I was a military commander when Trujillo was cleaning latrines as a Second Lieutenant. He stepped on me to get to the top. Now it is my time."

"Uh huh," says Josh. "So, this is nothing personal."

"Oh, it's *very* personal," says Borgatti. "You humiliated me in public. *No one* does that and goes on living. And so, to business." One of the goons tosses Borgatti a nasty looking braided leather bullwhip that he catches in his right hand. In a single motion, Borgatti unfurls the whip and cracks it next to Josh's head. The other goon hands Borgatti that scary looking Bowie knife from the Club Mojito. Borgatti flashes his lizard-grin at Josh as he moves toward him. Josh grabs one of the chairs, and the two start circling each other.

Cool Papa nudges me, and we both make a move to help Josh, but the two goons jump in front of us. At least if they're watching us they won't be able to gang up on Josh.

So it's a man with a bullwhip and a Bowie knife against a man with a wooden chair. Josh whips around and smashes the chair against craggy wall, and suddenly he's holding a chair leg with a jagged, rusty steel nail sticking out one side. Borgatti snaps the whip at Josh and wraps it around the chair leg, but then he gets a big surprise. He thinks he'll whip that chair leg out of Josh's hand, but he doesn't reckon on how strong Josh is. Josh uses the chair leg to jerk the whip out of Borgatti's hand. Borgatti lunges at Josh with the knife, but Josh dodges him as he shakes the whip loose from the chair leg and kicks it into a corner.

The two keep circling each other. Borgatti jabs at Josh, then springs for the kill, but Josh swings the chair leg in front of his chest, catching the knife. Borgatti jerks it out of the wood and slashes at Josh, who reels backwards, using that chair leg as a kind of sword. One of the goons backs away from us, edging over to the corner of the cell so he can grab the bullwhip. Cool Papa nods at me, and we split up so the one goon left to watch us can't guard us both. The goon chooses Cool Papa, which leaves me to help Josh without getting myself stabbed.

The other goon has grabbed the bullwhip and wants to toss it to Borgatti, but Borgatti is still circling Josh, and doesn't want to take his eyes off him. Every time Borgatti turns his eyes for a split second, Josh swings that chair leg at him. I creep toward this action lookin' for a chance.

It comes when Borgatti finally turns to catch the whip. I leap in between them and grab it instead. Josh swings at Borgatti with all his might, and "nails" him in his left arm. Borgatti shrieks in pain and slashes the Bowie knife wildly, slicing Josh's right leg. Josh's uniform blooms red with blood. Both Josh and Borgatti freeze, and then back away from each other. Josh collapses backwards on the floor.

The goons move in on Josh to finish him off. "This is it," I think to myself, but then something funny happens. Borgatti waves at his goons so they'll back off. He's holding his hand over the hole in his arm to staunch the flow of blood. "You have lost, Señor Gibson."

"Still alive," says Josh.

"Yes, for now. But you will die like all the others. Tonight, I think. I have a very special death planned for you. Before you die, you must know everything." Borgatti turns and walks out of the cell. The goons lock the cell door and march off right behind him.

Josh is a mess. Cool Papa rips off part of Josh's pant leg to make a bandage for the wound. "You did good, Josh," he says. "Leg of a chair 'gainst a bullwhip and a Bowie knife. You won by not dyin.'" Josh chuckles.

"Yeah, I guess," he says. "Tell me somethin', Papa."

"What do you want to know?"

"You believe in God?" asks Josh. Cool Papa laughs.

"I can't even figure out what *Satchel Paige* is up to, man. How am I gonna wrestle with a cat as mysterious as the Almighty?"

"Good answer. How 'bout you, Peanut?" I think back on that pasture back in Alabama, how I prayed for a miracle and the Lord delivered.

"I don't know. Not sure. But I guess so. I prayed one time, and I got what I wanted," I say.

"That's a good answer too," says Josh. "I like that. I feel a powerful need to talk to the Lord, if the two of you don't mind." We smile at Josh. Fine with us. Josh closes his eyes and lowers his head. "Lord, you and me gotta talk." He tries to sit up but can't. He groans and starts to fall backwards. Cool Papa slides over behind him so that he keeps Josh from hitting the floor.

"Take it easy, Josh," he says. Josh nods his thanks and keeps going.

"Lord, I can't say I'm your best customer. I've always tried not to bother you with the little stuff, or even a lot of the big stuff. I know you put me down here and made me what I am for some damn reason. I can feel you inside me every time I'm on that ball field, it just feels so…so right." He stops here. I look at Cool Papa who just stares at Josh.

"Keep goin'," whispers Cool Papa. Josh raises his head to ceiling, eyes still closed.

"If I AM here for a reason, I can't believe it's to let a bunch of evil men use me as a punching bag and a pincushion before they murder me for no good reason at all. Help me, Lord. From the bottom of this poor sinner's heart, help me. Help all of us. We're here by your grace and your mercy. Help us." And with that Josh slumps backwards into Cool Papa's arms, out cold.

"Anything you want to add?" asks Cool Papa. I ponder for a second, and look up at the ceiling myself.

"Lord, I recollect that when I asked you for that miracle earlier, I said I'd never ask for another one. I goofed up, 'cuz right now we're in a jam that's even worse. So I don't pretend this is the last time I'll ever ask for a miracle, but please, please, please show us a way out of this mess. Help Josh. Help Cool Papa. Help me."

"Amen, brother," says Cool Papa. "Good job. Now let's get some shut-eye so the Lord can help us work all this out."

CHAPTER TWENTY-FOUR

October 15, 1937

I'm deep in a dream when I'm shocked awake by a steel-toed boot kicking me in the side. Owww! I look up and see the tip of a shiny rifle bayonet pointed right at my nose. "You will come with us," barks Commandante Borgatti. The same soldiers who were here earlier are rousting Cool Papa and Josh. We're marched out to an Army troop truck and shoved in the back. Josh is hobbling pretty badly but won't let anyone help him. After we seat ourselves on the splintery wooden benches, four soldiers jump in after us, followed by Borgatti himself. Then we start bumping down the dirt road from the prison to wherever they're taking us.

"Good morning," says Borgatti. "Do not fear. Soon your misery will be ended. Our next stop will be your last."

"Uh huh," says Josh. "If that's so, I got a question."

"Certainly, Señor Gibson. Ask anything you wish." Señor Borgatti has a cheery smile to go with those dead eyes of his.

"You're gonna kill us, I know that," says Josh.

"I'm certainly going to kill you. The fate of your compatriots has yet to be determined," says Borgatti.

"What I want to know is, why did your boss Trujillo bring us down here? If he's so 'greatly beloved,' why does he need to win this series so bad? Underwood said something about some terrible thing that Trujillo did, and you were a part of it. What was that?" asks Josh, staring right at him. Borgatti's expression turns from a smile to a smirk.

"Ah. Yes. I believe it's time you knew the truth. The pity is that none of this has anything to do with you. It has to do with our enemy, the vile filth of Haiti."

"Haiti?" asks Josh, puzzled.

"The Dominican Republic shares this island with Haiti. This is most unfortunate. The Dominican people are noble, righteous and civilized – very much like the Caucasian peoples of Europe and America. Haiti, on the other hand, is a land of filthy black animals…very much like you and your teammates." He leans on this last phrase, and I get a sick feeling in the pit of my stomach as I watch Josh and Cool Papa wince.

"We were good enough for El Presidente to drag our asses over here to win him some ballgames," says Cool Papa.

"If you had *won* your ballgames, you wouldn't be riding in this troop truck," says Borgatti. "Señor Paige embodies the qualities that make the Haitian people so loathsome. Like them, he is greedy, lazy, and disloyal."

"Where do you people get stuff like that?" asks Josh.

"Stuff like that? By that do you mean, 'the truth'? Our exalted benefactor has studied the racial theories of the Chancellor of Germany, Adolf Hitler. Our leader's plans for the racial purification of the Dominican will proceed along the same lines as what Hitler is planning for Europe," says Borgatti. Never knew the Klan had an outpost in the Dominican, but I guess they're everywhere. Dang.

"So this terrible thing that happened had something to do with the Haitians," says Josh.

"Some naïve Americano sugar plantation owners had invited Haitian workers across our border to help harvest their crops. These Haitians abused our hospitality. They stole our sugar cane, menaced our women, and infected our people with the madness of pagan voodoo. El Presidente ordered me to rid our country of this filth. And so I did. I have cleansed the nation of this plague."

"When you say 'cleansed'…" says Josh.

"Yes, that's right, Señor Gibson. Just what you think." Borgatti smiles. We've come to the punchline of his sick joke. "The Haitian intruders have been eliminated. The Guardia Nacional, on my orders, have taken care of the Haitian problem. With machetes."

"How many you kill?" asks Josh in a low voice. Borgatti leans in toward him.

"Many thousands. Seventeen thousand, give or take," says Borgatti. Only then do I begin to understand what has happened. 17,000 people murdered! Hacked to death with machetes! I can't get my mind around this.

"Do your people know about this?" asks Cool Papa.

"Our Exalted Benefactor owns the newspapers and radio stations, Señor Bell, so the answer is no. The Norteamericanos – Señor Underwood and his friends – *they* know. And, of course, if they win the series and the election, they will twist this patriotic act to destroy El Presidente. But they will have no evidence."

"No evidence?" asks Josh. "How'd you work that?" Now Borgatti's evil smile becomes a full-on devil grin.

"Because *you*, Señor Gibson, are going to assist us in getting rid of the last of the bodies. And then you and your associates will join them. You will be the last of the last." Josh looks at Cool Papa, and then at me as Borgatti continues. "I'm sure you can understand how little your deaths will matter. When you join this great mass of Haitian dead, it will be like pouring a cup of water into the ocean."

The truck stops on the beach, and a horrible stench fouls the sweet sea breeze. A powerful urge comes over me to shut my eyes and hold my nose, but an even more powerful urge makes me turn my head and see where that smell is coming from. The honey-light of the full moon illuminates the horror. Dead bodies. Tons of them, piled on the beach like slabs of black beef. Sullen, bare-chested Guardia Nacional soldiers use pitchforks to load them onto a huge ocean barge. When I let my mama haul me to the Macedonia Baptist Church on Bedford Avenue in Pittsburgh, Pastor Odell Honeycutt loved to tell us what would happen if we approached the Great Throne of Judgment and were found unworthy to enter. We would be hurled into the pit of damnation, where we would understand the horror of being separated from a merciful God, and suffer for eternity. A world of never-ending torment, with no relief. I heard the words then, but I never really got what Hell was like. Now I know. I'm in it.

"Welcome to Death's Head Beach. Come, Señor Gibson. The sharks are hungry." With that, Borgatti grabs a shotgun and nods to the youngest soldier in the truck, who turns his bayonet on Josh. Josh hobbles off the truck. The other soldiers push us off and we follow along.

As we walk toward the barge, I come up alongside Josh. He looks down at me and smiles. Actually smiles! "Aren't you scared, Josh?" I ask, amazed.

"Listen here, Peanut," he murmurs as we walk toward that death barge. "Borgatti can take my freedom. He can shoot me, stab me, even cut me up and feed me to the sharks. But..." He drills me with those black eyes as the smile turns serious. *"He can't take my soul unless I give it to him, and I ain't gonna do that no matter what.* I didn't sell my soul to Underwood for money, and I'm not giving it to Borgatti by making me afraid of what's he gonna do to me. If I'm gonna die, I'm gonna die like a *man*. No more fear. No more runnin' from problems."

"Stand up for what's right." I echo words he said earlier.

"Yeah, somethin' like that," says Josh, looking ahead toward the barge. "Like you did with Satch when you turned down all that money. Made me proud, Peanut. So how are you feelin'?"

"Not so good, Josh." I feel light-headed, numb. Like a bad dream where I can't wake up.

"Borgatti is fixin' to kill all three of us. You think that's gonna happen?"

"I…I'm not sure." Only I am sure. We're doomed.

"Don't believe it. We're gonna get outta this. I made your mama a promise to take care of you, and I'm gonna keep that promise."

"How?" I can't tell is if he's givin' me gospel truth or tryin' to make me feel better.

"Don't know that, " says Josh, "and maybe I'm crazy. But there's something about the whole way Borgatti is doin' this that makes me think I can beat him. He's had a million chances to kill us already, you know? He's so full of himself he wants some kind of fight to the death so he can show the world how great he is. Like with Satchel, it's all about showin' the world he's number one. If he just gives me one clean shot at him..."

Another wave of nauseating funk wafts over us as we get closer to the barge. There are so many dead bodies on the barge that it groans under the weight, barely bobbing above the water line. Borgatti's main man jabs Josh with the bayonet and he walks the gangplank, followed by Cool Papa and me. Borgatti smiles at us. "One final, delightful surprise for you, Señor Gibson."

"What's that?" says Josh. Borgatti nods to a Guardia Nacional goon on the barge, who turns and nods to the cabin. The cabin door opens, and a second goon comes out holding a prisoner. Julissa Perez. Bruised. Bound. Terrified, but still defiant. Just when you think things can't possibly get any worse...

"Josh!" she screams. The goon backhands her, snapping her head sideways and dropping her to the filthy deck of the barge. The first goon stands her up as the second puts his bayonet in her back.

"Why..." stutters Josh.

"Because she humiliated me. Oh, and one other thing. She's a traitor," says Borgatti.

"Traitor?"

"One of my men caught her with that little camera of hers trying to film all this," he says, pointing at the mountain of bodies.

"What?" says Josh. He's dazed. He can't make sense of this.

"This film she is making – it is not a record of Trujillo's greatness. It is a gun to kill El Presidente."

"And YOU!" screams Julissa. Borgatti chuckles.

"Yes. Of course. Me as well. But all that ends here. You will die, and I will win. I *always* win." Borgatti nods to the goon behind the controls. This goon pushes the throttle and we put out to sea. No matter how much sea air washes over the barge, the stench stays on us. After ten minutes of calm seas I notice the water start to get choppy, and then I see why. Shark snouts. Hundreds of 'em bobbing up everywhere, sensing a meal. "Feeding time," says Borgatti. "Fascinating animal, the shark. Amazing sense of smell, much better than we humans. A shark can smell a single drop of blood in millions of gallons of sea water. They will do *anything* to survive, Señor Gibson. Like me. In my next life I will certainly be a shark."

"You got that right," mumbles Josh, and Borgatti chuckles.

"Time to go to work, Señor Gibson." He motions toward a pitchfork. "The sharks are waiting. You will pitch all these bodies into the water. My loving wife will be thrown to the sharks next to last. And yours will be the final body."

"Why don't you just shoot me now and get it over with?" asks Josh as his huge hands wrap themselves around the pitchfork handle.

"Shoot you?" says Borgatti, filled with mock surprise. "I'm not going to shoot you. You're going to pitch Julissa to the sharks while she's still alive, and then I'm going to push you into the water so that *you're* still alive when the sharks get you. So you can know what it's like to be ripped apart. And the last thing you'll ever see will be my face smiling at you as you're eaten alive."

Josh is holding the pitchfork, but he hasn't started pitching bodies into the ocean yet. He just stares at Borgatti. "I can't think of a single reason to help you out. No matter what I do, you're gonna kill us. I think I'm done here," says Josh. Borgatti's face hardens.

"I am willing to shoot you if you disobey," he says, leveling the shotgun at his chest. And then Josh shocks us all by tossing the pitchfork, handle first, at Borgatti. There's a split second where Borgatti has the chance to save himself – bat away the pitchfork with the rifle barrel, whip it back around and blow a hole in Josh. But instead he panics. Without thinking, he tries to catch the pitchfork in one hand and hold the shotgun in the other. Cool Papa dives down and rolls under Borgatti's legs, buckling his knees and forcing him to tumble backwards. Borgatti lets go of both rifle and pitchfork. Now it's a free-for-all. I grab the handle of the pitchfork as Josh gets a grip on the barrel of the shotgun. Borgatti seizes the stock as he tries to stand. For one horrible moment it seems like he's going to yank the gun out of Josh's hands, but Josh isn't interested in a tug of war. He uses the stock as a battering ram and shoves the shotgun into Borgatti's chest. Borgatti stumbles backwards, trips on the barge's foot-high rubber guard barrier, and falls backwards with a hideous scream into the ravenous school of sharks. The scream echoes until it's drowned out by the thrashing and the feeding frenzy. All five of us – Josh, Cool Papa, Julissa, me, and the goon piloting the barge – just stand there for the minute it takes for this to play out until all that's left is more bobbing shark noses and an oily crimson scum on the water.

Josh is still holding the stock of the shotgun. Now he turns it on the barge pilot as the three of us move in on him. The pilot is terrified. He lets Cool Papa take his pistol. "Back to shore," is all Josh says to him as I move to untie Julissa.

In the ten minutes it takes us to chug back to shore, the four of us try to figure out what to do next. "Borgatti's men will be waiting for you," says Julissa.

"Every one of those guys has a rifle," says Josh. "We killed their boss, and he's the big noise of the whole outfit."

"What are we gonna do?" I ask.

"Well," says Josh. "There's an outside chance that maybe they won't kill us on the beach. Maybe they're not as crazy as El Commandante. In which case we go back to prison, I guess."

"How many are we gonna face?" asks Cool Papa.

"I counted six when we pushed off," I say.

"All we got is one shotgun and one pistol," says Josh

"We start blazin' away, they'll kill us for sure," says Cool Papa.

"What do you think, Julissa?" asks Josh.

"I think it's a miracle we're still alive. Let's hope for another miracle."

"Damn straight," says Josh. "Let's play it cool and take our chances." Josh looks down at me and smiles. He's been right so far. He said he'd take care of me, and he has. And how.

The barge nears the shore and one of the six Guardia Nacionals uses a barge pole to bring it close to the dock. They know something's wrong, since the bodies are still on the barge. All six train their rifles on us. The Lieutenant in charge, a grizzled guy about Gus Greenlee's age, looks around for El Commandante Borgatti. When he doesn't see him, he fixes his glare on Josh.

I jump off the boat first, followed by Cool Papa, Julissa, and then Josh. Josh shocks the Lieutenant by handing him Borgatti's shotgun. "Señor Borgatti won't be needing this any longer." The Lieutenant swivels his head toward the barge pilot, who nods at him.

"You mean that you…that you and he…that El Commandante Borgatti is…is dead?" he asks, frowning.

"That's right," says Josh. Every rifle barrel turns toward Josh.

"And you…you were the one who…"

"Señor Borgatti took me out there to kill me. Kill all of us. He had that shotgun, I had a pitchfork. We fought. He got sloppy. He lost," says Josh.

One of the soldiers behind the Lieutenant, a kid about three years older than me, asks, "Where is his body?"

"Not really sure. In the stomach of a shark is my best guess," says Josh. "Ain't no way he's coming back here, if that's what you're thinking. Now I've got a question for you fellas."

"What?" asks the Lieutenant, still stupefied by the news of his boss's death.

"What are you fixin' to do with us?" And then the damndest thing happens. The Lieutenant looks at his men. They look back at him. Slowly, carefully, they put down their rifles. So what's it gonna be, hand to hand combat? The Lieutenant looks Josh square in the eye, and reaches out his hand. Josh looks at it, looks at the face of the Lieutenant, then takes it. They shake. No jive. My jaw practically bounces off the hard-packed mud on the beach. We're all in shock.

"Señor Gibson, you have our deep and profound thanks," says the Lieutenant.

"Thanks?" mutters Josh, nearly speechless.

"We are not blind, deaf, and dumb," says the Lieutenant. "We are well aware that Señor Borgatti was an evil man."

"Yeah, but..." says Josh.

"We hated him almost as much as you. The entire reason we are out here doing the devil's work is because we refused to cooperate with the killing of the Haitians. This was Borgatti's punishment – to make us dispose of the bodies. We strongly suspect – in fact, we are certain – that when we finished our task, he was planning to feed us to the sharks as well."

"What's going to happen when you take us back and Trujillo finds out..." but before Cool Papa can finish his sentence, a pudgy, light-skinned soldier with thick black hair falling in his eyes pipes up.

"As far as Trujillo knows, you're still in prison. We'll tell him that Borgatti was going to feed you to the sharks, when...ummmm..." I can see him trying to come up with a plausible whopper.

"Tell my father that Borgatti was hexed by a Haitian voodoo sorcerer," says Julissa.

"Right!" says the Lieutenant. "The sorcerer turned him into a zombie, and marched him into the sea. We were powerless to stop him."

"Wow!" I say. "You think anybody'll believe that?"

"The Exalted Benefactor believes even worse things about the Haitians," says Julissa. "This will set his imagination on fire."

One more surprise, although I'm surprised that I'm surprised by this. Every one of these fellas is a "Fanatico Loco" – a baseball nut with a big bet on the Dominican national team. They know everything about Josh, Cool Papa and Satchel. They tell us that the series is tied at 2-2 now, because Satchel pitched the Sugar Kings to a 3-Zip shutout while we were locked up. And the fifth game is this afternoon! And the Dominican team has no chance without Josh and Cool Papa!

CHAPTER TWENTY-FIVE

Josh is so sick and beaten down he can't even sit up in the troop truck on the way to the ballpark. He has to lie down on the splintery wood planks of the truck bed. I kneel behind him, holding his head while Julissa rips a piece of the pant leg of Cool Papa's uniform to use as a fresh dressing for Josh's leg. I'm worried he's not going to make it, but having Julissa smile down at him as she dabs his clammy forehead with some leftover cloth seems to perk him up.

"What Borgatti said..."

"About what?" asks Julissa.

"That film you're makin'..."

"Yes, he's right. I love my people, Josh. What he said..."

"Your film is a gun to kill Trujillo," says Josh.

"Yes, that's it. Imagine what would happen to him if the world could see what you saw. Of course, if he knows what I'm up to..."

"Think he does?"

"Not sure. I hope not. We should know soon. Now you get some rest, my love."

We finally bump up to the ballpark two hours later. Since a member of the Guardia Nacional is driving the truck, the Guardia Nacional at the ballpark gate opens it up for us. We drive onto the field, right up to the Dragones dugout.

Cool Papa jumps out first, followed by Julissa, and then yours truly. Then we help Josh hobble toward the bench. Only then do I look around and see the stage where the final act of this drama is gonna play itself out.

It is October 15, 1937, 5:13 p.m. 91 degrees, with a light ocean breeze from the southeast that is ruffling the hundreds of pennants, banners and flags planted everywhere. Some just have a picture of Trujillo's hangdog face. Some say "Re-Elect the Great Benefactor." Some show Trujillo's face in front of a shadow of an angel, over the words "God In the Sky, Trujillo On The Earth."

Soldiers – Trujillo's Elite Presidential Guard – ring the entire field. They're in their finest dress khakis, with silver helmets and bolt action rifles. They're not facing the fans to stop a riot if the Dragones blow it. They're facing the field, and a bunch of them are "protecting" our dugout. El Presidente does not lose.

Julissa's cameras are everywhere. That's good.

41,286 "Los Fanaticos Locos" have been sitting, standing, betting, swearing, laughing, drinking, and screaming for the two hours and thirteen minutes since the first pitch. You'd think they'd be exhausted by now, but the minute Josh shows himself in his filthy, bloody uniform, they let out a whoop that rattles the rafters of that old ballpark. I'm blinded by the glint of thousands of gold and silver coins passing hands as bets are placed on the final outcome of the final game.

Trujillo is on his golden throne, surrounded by the same group as usual, with Dr. Enrique Aybar on his right. Aybar's smile is a little bigger than usual now that Josh has arrived. He whispers in Trujillo's ear. From what I can see, we're his last hope. Why? I look at the scoreboard.

Sugar Kings – 1
Dragones – 0

Bottom of the 9th, two outs. Booker Samuels is on third, Bullet Hampton on second, Flash Fowler on first. Satch is on the mound in his Sugar Kings uniform. He's glaring at us as Deacon Powell runs out of the dugout.

"Where in the hell have you…" The Deacon stops as he sees Josh. "Oh my lord Jesus Christ in heaven above," he says, turning to me. "What happened?"

"Too much to tell," I say. "Borgatti threw us in prison, tried to murder us, only Josh…" Before I can tell the Deacon how Josh saved our lives, Josh delivers what good news there is to tell.

"Can't run a lick. Can barely walk. But I can hold a bat, if you need me."

"Damn right we need you," says Deacon. "Bullet Hampton has kept us in this thing, but Satch has shut our guys down completely. He's been razor sharp till this inning. We got a bunt single and he walked two guys, but nobody's hit a ball out of the infield."

"He's gettin' tired," I say. Everyone looks at me, with that "never underestimate Satch" look. "Maybe. A little." All eyes turn to Satch, who is playing catch with Choo-Choo Diaz to stay loose.

"One thing you ought to know," adds the Deacon. "Doctor Aybar paid us a little visit in the dressing room before the game." He nods toward the soldiers on the field. "He told us what was going to happen to us if we didn't bring glory to the Dominican people by achieving a…what were the words he used…'a sublime tidal wave of victory, that our Exalted Benefactor could ride to electoral triumph.'"

"Lemme guess," says Josh, grimacing. "We get a handshake, a ham sandwich, and a ticket on a tramp steamer back to the States." Deacon laughs and shakes his head.

"We get a ticket, alright," says the Deacon. "A one-way ticket to an open trench in the local pauper's graveyard."

"Uh huh," says Josh, staring at the hundreds of soldiers on the field. I'm sure he's thinking what I'm thinking. Every single one of those soldiers already has his orders. He won't even have to look at El Presidente if our guys blow this one. Just ready, aim, fire, and then...what? Feed us to the sharks, probably.

"You did say you can hold a bat, right?" says the Deacon.

"That's about it," says Josh.

"You get a base hit, I'll carry you around the bases myself."

I run to the dugout to grab Josh's bat. All the fellas look at me, and suddenly I remember that I'm covered with dirt, grime and blood just like Josh and Cool Papa. Willie Tatum hands me the bat. Nobody says a word. Everyone knows what's going to happen if Satch blows Josh away.

I hand the bat to Josh. He smiles at me. "You think I can get this done, Peanut?"

"I think you were put on earth to do this, Josh." He chuckles.

"Yeah. Me too." He turns and hobbles toward home plate, using the bat as a cane. As he gets ready to step in, I turn and look at the grandstands.

The Exalted Benefactor himself, Rafael Trujillo, is on his feet in front of his golden throne, with Dr. Aybar whispering in his ear. The two of them are surrounded by a hundred soldiers, all turned to the crowd behind them. They are ready to fight their way out.

On the other side of the field is Tyler Underwood, holding a huge tropical drink in one hand and a cigarette in the other. He's surrounded by his own bunch of rifle-bearing security guys, but he looks like he doesn't think he'll need them. He's smiling. I think he's already picking out the drapes for the Presidential Palace so it'll be all set when he moves in.

The ump yells "Play ball!" but Josh and Satch just stare at one another. This is the moment each has waited for. "PLAY...BALLLLLLLL!" screams the ump directly into Josh's ear. This breaks the spell. I can see Josh grimace as he plants his right foot in the back of the box, then his left foot, and then he moves his right hand up his left arm, only there's no sleeve left to push up. Satch stares in to get his sign...and then asks for time out. Josh steps out of the box.

I got to hand it to Satch – the man's got nerve. He turns around, and waves at his outfielders. He's ordering them to come in. That is so Satchel. He's pushing all his chips into the middle of the poker table, along with the mortgage on his house and the keys to his car. True to form, Trujillo starts jawing at Dr. Aybar and, on the first base side, Underwood rears backwards and horse laughs.

Now the outfielders are sitting on the infield grass. The infielders have to stay put because of the three men on base. Satch turns back to Josh and motions with his hand to step in, which Josh does – back foot, front foot, phantom sleeve. I suddenly notice – the ballpark is completely pin-drop quiet. Not a peep. It's like the whole world is holding its breath.

This is it. This is the showdown. Finally, after two breathers, the unstoppable force is gonna try to bulldoze the immovable object.

Satch ain't smiling. In fact, he looks like a demon out there, staring daggers at Josh under hooded eyes. Just a single wind-up this time. Satch rears back and fires. Josh swings – and misses. "Stee-rike one!" screams the umpire, and a bellow – half cheer, half groan – goes up from the stands. Josh collapses to one knee, then pushes himself back up with his bat. He grimaces with every move.

Waves of gold and silver flash as coins pass from hand to hand, and the fans buzz as Josh stands back in for the next pitch. Satch checks Booker Samuels dancing off third base, then windmills once and unleashes a big ol' bat dodger curveball that starts at Josh's head, then bends down and nips the inside of the plate. BIG SWING...and miss as Josh yelps in pain and drops his bat. This time I hear more groans than cheers. Josh is bent over, hands on knees, staring at the dirt. Then he picks up the bat, rights himself, shakes his head to clear it, and climbs back in.

Same drill – Satch checks Booker on third, rears back, and fires – straight at Josh's head. Josh leans his head back. The ball grazes the bill of his cap and spins it sideways. "HIT BY PITCH! TAKE YOUR BASE!" screams the umpire as he jumps out from behind home plate and points at first. The game's tied! Or is it? Josh turns and looks at the ump. The ump steps back and looks at Trujillo. Josh and Satch both look at Trujillo. Trujillo nods at the ump, who yells, "BALL ONE!" as he gets back behind the catcher. But before Satch can toe the rubber Josh backs out and motions for me to bring him a towel.

I run it up to him, and man does he need it, 'cuz he's drenched in sweat. He wipes his face and says, "What do ya think, Peanut?"

"'Bout what?" I ask.

"What's the next pitch?"

"I don't know." Holy cow! Is Josh asking me for hitting advice? If so, we're in a heap of trouble.

"Every time Satch comes high and tight, what happens next?" asks Josh. I think for a moment, then it comes to me.

"Fast ball. Down and away," I say.

"Exactly. You know that. I know that, and Satch *knows* that I know it. And I know that Satch knows that I know it. So do you think that's what he's gonna do? Throw me the pitch I'm expecting?" The ump is looking at us. He wants Josh back in the box and this thing over with.

"Yeah, I do. Down and out fastball is Satch's best pitch. He's gonna dare you to hit it. Knowing that you know what's coming will make it sweeter when he strikes you out. He'll brag about it on his deathbed."

"Good boy," says Josh, smiling. "You've been payin' attention. Your mama ain't raising no fool." He tosses the towel back to me. "Now excuse me, I got some unfinished business to take care of. We gotta see who really is the best of the best."

I run back to the dugout. "What was that about?" asks Deacon Powell.

"How much money you got on you, Deacon?" I ask.

"'Bout 20 bucks American," he says.

"Give it to Payday. Put it on Josh," I say.

Everybody in that ballpark – Trujillo, Aybar, Tyler Underwood, the soldiers, everybody – cranes his head forward. Josh stares at Satch, who stares back. Josh plants his right foot, then his left, then pushes up the sleeve that ain't there. Now he's ready.

Satch doesn't even look at Booker on third. Booker dances toward the plate as Satch windmills once, then grunts as he puts everything he's got into the pitch -- a pure, smokin' blazer, fading away from Josh's knees on the far side of the plate, painting the black on the outside. A perfect pitch. And Josh, in that clean, one-piece swing, steps right into it. KA-BOOM! Everyone on the field turns and watches as the ball rifles over the second baseman's head. It actually seems to rise higher and higher as it sails past the center fielder, over the red and blue banner that says "Re-Elect The Great Benefactor," and clean over the bleachers. It looks to me like it's still going up as it disappears into the sky over the cane fields behind the ballpark.

And now the eruption. Every fan becomes part of a great, single beast, roaring with joy as it bursts from chains that held it down. And the ear-splitting roar only gets louder as Josh, who stood at home plate and watched his awesome handiwork, drops his bat and starts lurching around the bases. Satch is turned around, still staring at the spot where the ball cleared the fence. He absolutely will not look at Josh as Josh shambles around him and the other three runners touch home plate.

When Josh touches third, Cool Papa is there to shake his hand. Then the sky opens up with a heavenly shower – millions and millions of silver and gold raindrops. Seems like every fan in that ballpark has joined the celebration, throwing fistfuls of coins onto the field. Josh is actually laughing as he comes up to home plate. With Cool Papa at his side, he stops just short, and looks toward the dugout. He's waving at me! I run out to join him. He takes my hand, and we cross home plate together. Then Josh turns toward the fans and opens his arms. The cheers had been dying, but the beast roars again as Josh smiles and closes his eyes against the downpour of coins.

He looked death in the face and stared it down.

He did the right thing when it could have cost him his life.

He showed the world who the best ballplayer in the world really is.

This is his moment. He knows who he really is. And so do I.

"Get ready, fellas!" screams Cool Papa as we're all swept up by a squad of Trujillo's elite guard. These soldiers are the best of the best – the ones that El President trusted to guard his box, and save his life if the Dragones lost the game. Now they're herding everyone toward the middle of the diamond as the rest of the soldiers guard the field, trying to stop Los Fanaticos Locos from jumping the railings and blitzing the celebration. Three soldiers have the drop on Satch, pushing him with their bayonets into the crowd of Dragones. Dr. Aybar is in the middle of this mix. He bustles up to Satchel in the midst of this chaos. "Señor Paige, I must know something before our Beloved and Exalted Benefactor addresses our people," he says.

"What's that?" asks Satchel, still dazed at being beaten.

"Why did you betray El Presidente? Why did you jump to the Sugar Kings? You must have known your efforts could have denied the Dominican people the enlightened leadership of El Presidente Trujillo. Were you bribed?" Satch tries to open his mouth, but all he can see are the angry soldiers behind Aybar, itching to use their rifles on a traitor. Do the right thing, Peanut. Now or never.

"OR," I pipe up, "were you *forced* by Tyler Underwood to join the Sugar Kings?"

"Forced?" asks Satch. He's got a look of panic in his eyes. What's this about? I move in next to them.

"Forced," I repeat. "You know, Satch. Against your will."

"Huh?" asks Satch. Everything's happening fast, and Satch can't quite catch up, but Cool Papa can see what's goin' down.

"We all swore to win these games for El Presidente and the Dominican people, didn't we?" asks Cool Papa.

"Yeah, but..." says Satch. I knife in before Satch can get himself sideways with Aybar.

"So, the *only possible reason* you'd betray this oath..." I begin.

"Which you took very seriously, didn't you?" asks Cool Papa.

"Ummmm, sure," says Satchel, lying through his teeth.

"...is if Underwood and the sugar combine *kidnapped you* and *forced you* to play for the Sugar Kings. *Right*?" I've done my best. Finally I see a big light bulb go on over Satchel's head. He turns to Aybar.

"Yeah! Yeah, that's it! Exactly! The fact is, Doc," says Satch, "that – yeah, what Peanut said. Satchel was grabbed by those sugar guys."

"Held against your will," I say.

"That's right," says Satch.

"Told that if you didn't play for the Sugar Kings, they'd kill you, and your family back in the states," says Cool Papa. He and I are both looking directly in the smiling face of Dr. Aybar. It's like the three of us are talking to each other without saying a word, and Satch is trying to get on our wavelength.

"That's just what happened," says Satchel.

"But you secretly stayed loyal to El Presidente, didn't you?" I say. Satch nods vigorously.

"Sure did," says Satch.

"Then why did you go against the wishes of El Presidente and win the fourth game for the Sugar Kings?" asks Cool Papa.

"Well...because...ummmm...." Satch sputters.

"BECAUSE," I say, riffing on what Cool Papa is laying down, "by winning the fourth game, that just made the fifth game more important!"

"So that VICTORY in the fifth game would be fresh in the minds of every Dominican voter," says Cool Papa.

"Exactly! Yes! That's just what Satchel did!"

"That's why you brought it all down to the final at bat with Josh," I suggest. Josh's ears perk up as he hears this. He's part of the conversation now.

"Sure! That's why I loaded the bases, too," agrees Satch.

"Every fan in that ballpark thought the Sugar Kings were going to win," says Cool Papa."

"Every one, yeah."

"Only you and Josh worked it out so that Josh would show up at the last possible moment," I say.

"You bet," says Satch.

"And then, to ensure that the Exalted Benefactor would reap the greatest benefit possible from this glorious victory, you threw Josh a fat pitch so that he would be sure to hit a home run," says Cool Papa.

"What?!?" screams Josh.

"YEAH!" yells Satch. "That's EXACTLY what happened, Dr. Aybar. Hell, I know Josh better than Josh knows himself. Satchel had the whole, entire thing mapped out in his head before it happened."

"AIN'T NO WAY you threw me a lollipop, Satch, and you know it!" screams Josh, and now Cool Papa moves right up into Josh's face.

"Calm down, Josh. Every single one of us knows what really happened." Cool Papa looks at Satch. "Don't we?" Satch stares at him, then at me, then nods. Cool Papa turns to Dr. Aybar. "Don't we?" Dr. Aybar nods as well.

"I believe," says Dr. Aybar, smiling at me, "I have just what I need to reassure El Presidente that his trust in the great Satchel Paige was not mis-placed. That this clever plan heightened the dramatic quality of the series. That what looked like treachery was in fact bravery in service to our cause."

"So Satch can be part of the celebration?" asks Cool Papa.

"Just so," says Dr. Aybar. "Señor Paige guaranteed victory at our first meeting, and a victory has been delivered. No more need be said." He turns and walks off with the disappointed clutch of soldiers right behind. Satch starts to open his mouth, but Cool Papa cuts him off.

"Before you say a thing, Satch, understand that Peanut here just saved your life. You understand that, don't you?" Satch looks wounded, but nods at me.

"Yeah."

Cool Papa turns to Josh. "Get over here." Now Satch, Josh, Cool Papa and I are in a tight group facing each other. "A lot's been said about who's the best, who can strike out who, and who can hit a home run off of who anytime he pleases. Don't matter what Trujillo thinks, what the fans here think, or what Aybar thinks. Only matters what *we* think, right? Because only the people standing *right here* will ever know the truth."

"Right," says Josh. Satch nods.

"So here's what I think, and tell me if you fellas agree with me. Satch, I think you wanted to strike out Josh more than you ever wanted anything else in the world, and you threw the nastiest pitch you had left in you. What was that pitch, Peanut?"

"Down and out heater with a monster hop," I say. "A 'bee ball' that buzzed just as nicely as you please."

"And Josh took your very best pitch way deep downtown," says Cool Papa, "and that settles the issue of who can beat who once and for all. You good with that, Satch?" Satchel is staring at the ground, scratching the dirt with the steel toe-plate of right shoe. "Satch?" says Cool Papa, a little louder. "I need you to answer me right now in front of Cool Papa, Josh, and Peanut, because I don't want to never hear *nothin'* in no newspaper about how you saved our lives in the Dominican by serving up a fat one to Josh in the bottom of the ninth, blah blah blah. There's *one hero* in this story, and for once *it ain't Satchel Paige.* Is it?"

"No," says Satch, in a faint whisper.

"What's that, Satch? I can't hear you," says Cool Papa. Finally, Satch looks up at Cool Papa.

"No," says Satch.

"This time Josh is the man," says Cool Papa.

"Yeah," says Satch.

"Say it," says Cool Papa. "To him. Say it to Josh." Satch finally looks at Josh. He takes a moment to gather himself.

"You got it done, my friend," says Satch. "What Cool Papa said. Satchel wanted to whiff your ass so bad he could taste it, so he'd have braggin' rights till the end of time. Didn't work out that way. You beat ol' Satch, straight up. You be the man." Satch sticks out his hand, and Josh shakes it.

Only now do I notice all the dead-serious frivolity erupting around us. Six of the Exalted Benefactor's finest are wheeling a gold-plated speaking platform onto the outfield grass behind second base. More soldiers are helping Julissa move three newsreel cameras into place. The Dominican national merengue marching band strikes up the national anthem as it high-steps toward the podium, with El Presidente himself matching Dr. Aybar step for step as they both stride behind the last two rows of conga drums. The band plays the usual highfalutin fanfare, like Trujillo is going to take his place next to God on a fluffy white cloud in heaven, and then Trujillo climbs up to the podium and waves to Los Fanaticos Locos, who scream their heads off but don't throw a single coin at him, because I guess they remember that Trujillo's picture is on the money anyway. "What's he gonna say?" I ask Cool Papa, as Deacon Powell joins us.

"First, he'll brag on himself and figure out some way to take credit for this whole thing," says Cool Papa.

"Then he'll lay that jive piece of hardware, the 'Trujillo Trophy' or some such, on us," says the Deacon.

"And then he'll brag on himself some more, and maybe thank us," says Cool Papa.

"Or maybe not," says the Deacon. "And then he'll finish by bragging on himself a third time and probably take credit for hitting Josh's home run."

"Sounds about right," I say as the cheers die down, and Trujillo steps up to the microphone. No movie studio in Hollywood could have planned this moment any better. The golden light of late afternoon makes him look like one of those idols the natives worship in jungle movies.

"¡Gracias, mis seres queridos!" says Trujillo. "¡Esta es TU victoria! Hice todo esto por ¡USTEDES!" He opens his arms to the crowd, and everyone goes wild. Cool Papa cocks his head toward me, and then he and the Deacon nod at each other. Bragging on himself, just like Cool Papa said. "Quiero que me acompañen el Señor Josh Gibson y el Señor Cool Papa Bell aquí en el podio, por favor." Trujillo waves the guys up to the podium. As Josh and Cool Papa climb up to stand by him, Dr. Aybar and two soldiers hoist that hideous "Trujillo Trophy" – the life-sized gold plated statue of the Exalted Benefactor leaning on a baseball bat – up next to him. "Señores," says Trujillo to the cameras, "Es mi gran honor presentar le a usted y sus compañeros de los Dragones con este premio por la victoria que han logrado para el pueblo Dominicano." Josh and Cool Papa smile as the movie cameras roll and news photographers grab flash pictures of them.

"Thanks," says Josh, and he and Cool Papa start to leave, only their way is blocked by Trujillo's Elite Guard.

"Not quite yet, gentlemen," says Trujillo quietly. He's smiling that nasty grin of his. "I have an announcement to make." Cool Papa perks up at this. Announcement? What's to announce?

"I got a bad feeling about this," says Deacon Powell. Me too.

As Trujillo steps up to the public address microphone, I say to the Deacon, "Tell me exactly what he says, word for word." The Deacon nods.

"Mis amigos....usted incluido Señor Paige, porque derrotándolo ha hecho esta victoria aun mas dulce..."

The Deacon grimaces as he stares at Trujillo, translating. "My friends, including Satchel Paige, because defeating you has made our victory all the sweeter..." I see Satch muster a sickly smile as he half-heartedly waves at the crowd.

Trujillo continues. He's on a roll, playing this for all its worth. "Gracias a esta magnífica victoria, y por lo que han hecho estos jugadores por mi, y porque el pueblo Dominicano - mis queridos niños - desean y merecen los mejores beisbolistas del mundo, he tomado una decisión."

The Deacon decodes it for me and Cool Papa. "Because of this magnificent triumph, and because of what these players have done for me, and because the Dominican people -- my beloved children -- crave and deserve the best baseball players in the world, I have made a decision." The Deacon looks at Cool Papa. Big, big trouble.

Trujillo is almost yelling into the microphone, he's so worked up. "Después de mi victoria en las urnas mañana, mi primer acto oficial en mi siguiente mandato será designar los Dragones de Ciudad Trujillo ¡COMO EL EQUIPO OFICIAL NACIONAL DE LA REPUBLICA DOMINICANA!"

The Deacon looks like a mule just kicked him in the gut. As the crowd screams and chants Trujillo's name, he gives it to us straight. "After my victory at the polls tomorrow, my first official act in my next term of office will be to designate the Ciudad Trujillo Dragones as the...the..." He gags on the words, so Cool Papa finishes the sentence.

"...permanent official national team of the Dominican Republic."

My heart drops into my shoes and my mouth dries up as the crowd goes absolutely crazy. We're his meal ticket to being president for life! We're NEVER gonna get off this damn island! He's gonna keep us here FOREVER! I look over at Josh, who is looking at Cool Papa. Neither one of them can believe it. But Trujillo ain't even done speechifyin'. He quiets the crowd, takes his voice down a notch, and smiles at his "beloved children."

"¡Mis seres queridos, imaginen nuestra gloria! Vamos a retar a los equipos de todo el mundo a que vengan aquí y jueguen contra este equipo invencible de beisbolistas inmortales en la única y verdadera 'Serie Mundia,' compuesto de los mejores equipos de todo el planeta. El equipo que seguro va ganar es NUESTRO equipo - un equipo que a partir de hoy será conocido como "Las Estrellas de Trujillo."

We all look at the Deacon. "Says he's gonna challenge teams from all over the world, and play 'em in a real 'world series.' Gonna call the team 'Trujillo's All-Stars.'"

The crowd erupts into cheers once more as Josh, Cool Papa, and Satchel move in on Dr. Aybar. I follow behind them.

"What's going on?" says Cool Papa, nose to nose with Aybar.

"I am as surprised as you are," says Aybar calmly, still with that little smile.

"This wasn't our deal!" screams Satchel. "We grab the gold ring, we vamoose."

"With all due respect, Señor Paige, I do not believe you are the best one to assume a stance of righteous indignation about the inviolate nature of agreements." Woo! Got him there. Satchel steps back, and Josh steps up.

"Doctor Aybar, what's going on? Is this just another bunch of blather to make sure El Presidente wins the election tomorrow? Is he really gonna keep us here another week? Or a month? Or...." Josh's last word falls off a cliff into a very dark pit of pessimism.

"I have been honest with you gentlemen from the first moment we met," says Aybar. "And I will be truthful yet again. Our Exalted Benefactor has not chosen to take me into his confidence on this matter. When he said that you would remain in our country to play as our national team, this was as big a surprise to me as it was to you."

"So he's serious?" asks Josh.

"I know El Presidente as well as anyone in this land of plenty. I believe, from his choice of words and his tone of voice, that he is completely serious. I believe that he means to honor you with this appointment, and that he will do whatever it takes to see that you accept his kind and generous offer."

"I say we call the American ambassador," says a defiant Satchel to the players. Then he turns to Aybar. "You guys can't keep us here against our will. That's slavery. That ain't right. Our country fought a damn

Civil War over that, and slavery lost." Aybar's smile disappears. He steps so close to Satchel I've got to lean forward to hear what he says.

"Slavery, Señor Paige?" Satchel stares at Aybar, and Aybar stares back. "My understanding is that you have already been paid many times your best yearly income to play for El Presidente's team. And you were paid even more to betray your first benefactor to play for the Sugar Kings."

"I'm sick of this place," says Satchel. "I want out." Aybar re-directs his gaze from Satchel to the whole team.

"Here is what will happen. You will return to your hotel for an evening of rest. Señor Gibson will receive medical attention for his leg. Tomorrow, thanks to your efforts on the ball field, the Dominican people will vote for El Presidente Trujillo, and he will continue to lead our people to glory. A magnificent celebration will then take place at El Presidente's home, and you are invited. There will be fine food and drink, music and many attractive young ladies. The American Ambassador will be there. At that time you may address your concerns to him, and to El Presidente. I only ask one thing before you do so."

"What's that?" spits Satchel. Aybar takes his time answering.

"I ask that you, Satchel, consult your teammates, Señor Josh Gibson and Señor Cool Papa Bell about their reasons for missing the fourth game of this series. I believe you will discover just *how serious* El

Presidente is about his plan, the enthusiasm he will employ to make sure that you accept his invitation, and the consequences you will suffer if you choose to decline his invitation. Until then, gentlemen…" And with that, Aybar walks off.

CHAPTER TWENTY-SIX

On the bus back to the hotel, Cool Papa tells the fellas what happened to us. He doesn't leave out anything – the prison, the news flash about the Haitians being killed, the fight, the sharks, the pitchfork, Borgatti's death – he tells the whole thing. Josh doesn't say a single word, but the way he looks – that says it all. By the time Cool Papa's done telling the tale, the fellas are dead quiet. Yes, even Satch is mute, but I know what he's thinking. He's thinking the same thing everyone else is thinking – we're here for life, or until El Presidente gets tired of his new toy, and then we might end up as shark chum.

Now it's midnight. I'm in bed. Josh is all patched up now -- Trujillo sent five doctors and eight nurses to fuss over him, so Josh can make the proper showing at El Presidente's rumpus. I think he's asleep. I'm wide-awake. Maybe it's the gunfire outside -- Los Fanaticos Locos are still running wild in the streets celebrating our big win over the Sugar Kings. Maybe it's something else. My mind is on fire. All I can think about is home. Will I ever see my mama again? I can see her face vivid in my mind, feel her hugs, smell her sweet perfume. Will I ever walk out onto Greenlee Field? Catch the new Errol Flynn picture at Loew's Penn? Will I ever suck in that smoky Pittsburgh air, have a two-scoop chocolate ice cream soda at the Rexall Drug, or put out another edition of the *Crawford Courier*? Dang, I got some great stories, but I might die with those stories still inside me! "Josh," I whisper. "You awake?"

"No, I'm sleepin'," he says.

"Then why..."

"Course I'm awake."

"What are you thinking about?"

"Thinking about how nice it would be if you'd go to sleep," he says. I ignore him.

"What are the chances of us staying here the rest of our lives?" Josh doesn't say anything for quite a while. About thirty seconds, or five gunshots.

"Peanut," he says, finally, "How am I doing so far?"

"What?" I ask.

"How am I doing? I told your mama I'd look after you. Everything okay so far?"

"Yeah, sure, Josh. Better than okay. You saved my damn life for about the twenty-fifth time."

"Don't use curse words."

"Sorry."

"Okay then," says Josh. "If I asked for a favor, would you help me out?"

"Anything!" I say quickly.

"Good," he says. "Here's what I want. No matter what happens for the next couple of days, trust me. Whatever I say or do, go with it."

"Trust you?"

"Yeah. Can you do that?"

"Yeah. I guess," I say, although I'm not quite sure what he really wants.

"We've had some bad things happen to us, and what's coming up may be even worse. You're gonna scratch your head a couple of times at what I'm doing, but it's all part of what I'm up to, okay?"

"What are you up to?" I ask.

"A kind of plan. It's all in my head. At least most of it. Some of it depends on what happens at El Presidente's jamboree."

"Can you tell me what you're thinking?"

"Better if you don't know. That's why I need you to trust me."

"Okay, Josh," I say. "What Satchel said. You're the man."

"Thanks, Peanut. Now go to sleep."

"Night, Josh."

"Night, Peanut." I shut my eyes and decide that I'm really, really going to do what Josh says. Trust him. Somehow, some way we're going to get out of this. I can almost taste that chocolate soda at the Rexall.

October 16, 1937

When morning comes, we both discover we have a full set of evening clothes hanging on the doorknob of the room. I'm talking black, double-breasted, peaked-lapel tuxedos for the both of us, with the works – silk shirt, cummerbund, bow tie, and gold cuff links. When I try on this monkey suit, I feel like the kid in that Errol Flynn movie who goes from being a pauper to being a prince, just like that. And you'd never know that Josh was on death's door two days ago. He looks like a fierce African King. Or Paul Robeson playing one.

Come sunset, all the fellas meet in the hotel lobby and show off their fancy new duds. Then the limousines pick us up and we tootle toward to Trujillo's palace. Fans line the streets, waving Dominican flags at us. The limo door opens, and we're deposited on a red carpet that leads to the door of the mansion. To get to that door we have to walk through a gauntlet of rifle-toting Guardia Nacional soldiers – must be two hundred of 'em on each side of us. Julissa pulls at the corners of her mouth -- "SMILE, FELLAS!" as her movie cameras capture our arrival.

When we walk in, everyone stops what they're doing and gives us a big round of applause. Satch and Josh are a study in opposites. Josh, who you'd think would still be mad at the way he was treated, is as sunny and cheerful as a baby-kissing Mayor running for re-election. He shakes the hands of the gents and hugs the ladies that want hugs. Satch, on the other hand, is a grumpus. He gives a "dead fish" handshake to those who won't take no for an answer, but the way he glowers scares off most everybody else.

I'm standing in line waiting for a server to dish me up another "Dominican flag" -- white rice, red beans, and fried green plantains – when Josh intercepts me. "You with me, Peanut?" he asks.

"All the way," I say.

"Got a job for you, then."

"Anything."

"I want you to keep an eye on Satch," says Josh. "Keep him outta trouble. I got some business to attend to."

"When you say keep an eye on him..."

"Follow him around. Grab somebody -- Cool Papa or the Deacon -- if it looks like he's getting' us into a mess." Before I object – like, how exactly am I supposed to stop Satch from doing anything, since nobody else ever has – Josh melts into the crowd. And as soon as Josh leaves, I see Satch make a beeline for a beefy, silver-haired white gent who is chatting up Dr. Aybar. Ten bucks says this is the United States Ambassador to the Dominican Republic. I'm also betting that Mount Satchel is about to erupt, and we're about to be swallowed in red-hot lava. I look around for Cool Papa.

"Hey, boss, a bunch of Americans need your help!" Satch yells as he trots up to the Ambassador, with me right behind him. The Ambassador is going to play it cool. He steps forward and sticks out his hand.

"Henry Norweb, Mr. Paige. Dr. Aybar here was telling me that..."

"You're the Ambassador, right?" says Satch, cutting him off.

"Yes, that's correct."

"Well, I want to report the biggest damn crime since the Lindbergh baby done got itself snatched."

Aybar frowns. "Señor Paige, I don't think..."

"A crime? What kind of crime?" asks Norweb.

"Kidnapping!" says Satchel.

"Really!" says Norweb. "Who has been taken?"

"I HAVE!" yells Satchel.

"You?" asks Norweb, baffled.

"Satch!" I say, but no one pays attention.

"There's an illegal criminal plot to keep Satchel Paige from going back to the United States," says Satch. Norweb turns Aybar.

"Is this true, Dr. Aybar?" Aybar turns to Satchel and bears down on him.

"Señor Paige, are you here of your own free will and volition..."

"No!"

"...because of an agreement with the government of the Dominican Republic to exchange your services for specified amounts of cash money..."

"Well..."

"...which have been paid in a timely fashion?"

"Satchel's been paid, yeah, but..." Satch is on the defensive now. Aybar leans in for the kill.

"Did you, in fact, *violate* this agreement with our government?"

"No! I mean, well, yeah, but only because..."

"DESPITE your gross violation – really a betrayal of our agreement, has anyone made *any attempt whatsoever* to interfere with your travel? *Anyone at all?"* Aybar just looks at Satch with that infuriating little smile of his. Satch can't take it any longer. He turns to Norweb.

"El Presidente himself said he's gonna keep us here! Everybody heard him! He 'decided' that we're his new national team. He's kidnapping us!"

"SATCH! SHUT UP!" I scream. No one even looks at me, because El Presidente is roaring up right behind me.

"I am INVITING you!" yells Trujillo. "Am I to understand that you are *accusing me of a crime,* Señor Paige?"

"No one's accusing anyone of anything," says Norweb, eager to keep a lid on this. But, of course, Satchel won't let it go.

"I AM accusing someone of something! I'm accusing *this cat right here,*" says Satch, pointing at Trujillo, "of keeping us here at *gunpoint*. When we want to leave. Which is, like, *right after this wingding."*

"So, if I understand you," says Aybar, "you are accusing the newly re-elected President of the

Dominican Republic of committing a crime...that will take place in the future."

"NEAR future," says Satch, "Like tomorrow morning."

"Well," says Ambassador Norweb, "I can't do anything about a crime that hasn't happened yet."

"So you're just gonna let 'em do it?" says Satchel to Norweb as he points at Trujillo. "You're just gonna let this crazy man feed a bunch of your countrymen to the sharks?" Everybody stiffens at this. Satch, as usual, has gone too far. I can practically see smoke coming out of El Presidente's ears.

"It never occurred to me to arrest Señor Paige until this very moment, but he is very close to slandering me. And when he slanders me, he slanders the Dominican people who have placed their trust in me to guide them. Señor Paige, I demand that you disavow your last statement and apologize to my countrymen." Satch opens his mouth so he can stick the other foot in, but another voice fills the room.

"We are your *guests*, El Presidente," booms Josh, walking up to the group with a great big smile on his face. Julissa and two others have those hand-held "Eyemo" cameras to catch all this. "I apologize for my hot-headed teammate Señor Paige," says Josh. "I apologize to the Dominican people. And I wonder if your kind and generous offer to become the national team of the Dominican Republic still stands?" My mouth drops open. What?!? Before I can say anything I remember my promise. I gotta trust him.

"Certainly, Señor Gibson," says Trujillo, smiling.

"Will you treat us with the same kindness and generosity you've shown us so far?" Josh's baritone voice turns every head in the room towards our group. Trujillo is grinning and nodding.

"You are gods of baseball. You will continue to be treated as such."

"In that case, we are proud to accept your invitation." Josh shakes Trujillo's hand, and then steps out to address the crowd. "Ladies and gentlemen, I came to your country as co-captain of the Pittsburgh Crawfords, to play in a simple five game tournament. I never imagined what would happen to me -- that I would fall in love with your country, and its people -- and especially its benevolent and exalted leader, El Presidente Rafael Trujillo." Josh pauses as the crowd cheers. Satchel looks sick, and the rest of the fellas look baffled. "I am no longer a member of the Pittsburgh Crawfords. I am now the Captain -- am I the Captain, Doctor Aybar?" Aybar smiles and nods.

"I hereby appoint you Captain, Señor Gibson."

"I am now *honored* to be the Captain of *Trujillo's All-Stars*, the *greatest baseball team in the world!*" An even bigger cheer erupts, and partygoers surge toward us, shaking our hands and patting our backs. "VICTORY!" shouts Josh.

"VICTORY!" shouts Trujillo.

"VICTORY! VICTORY! VICTORY!" chants the crowd. As Julissa and the two other cameras move into place, Josh grabs Trujillo's arm and yanks it skyward, like Josh just heard that Trujillo won the election. Satch grabs my arm and pulls me out of this crush.

"Has Josh lost his marbles?" asks Satch, poking me in the chest.

"I don't think so."

"He tell you he was goin' to sell us out like this?"

"No!"

"Well, you tell your pal Josh this from Ol' Satchel, okay, Peanut?"

"O-okay," I say as he backs me up against a wall.

"You tell Señor Josh Gibson that he and his new pals might be able to keep Satchel Paige on this godforsaken island for a little while, and he might be able even be able to get Satchel to the ballpark if he has enough brass knuckles, fire bombs and machine guns. But the *only way* Josh is gonna get Satchel out on that pitcher's mound is in a damn *casket*. He can take 'Trujillo's All-Stars,' fold it eight ways and *put it where the moon don't shine*."

CHAPTER TWENTY-SEVEN

What's amazing about the rest of the party is how exactly opposite Josh and Satchel have become since we landed here. It's like the Good Lord took what made Satchel special and put it into Josh, and then stuck the dark parts of Josh into Satchel. Josh is the life of the party, chatting up Trujillo, Trujillo's pals, and Trujillo's family. He makes conversation with everybody who thinks it will help them to hang with someone who knows Trujillo, which is everybody at the wingding. He coaxes Cool Papa into sitting in with the band -- Josh behind the drum kit, Cool Papa on congas. Josh even ventures out on the dance floor without being shoved. He dances the merengue with every female in the place, including Julissa and even Nova Quezada, the babe who was on Satch like moss on a rock when we first got here.

Satch, on the other hand, is Gloomy Gus. He sulks in a corner, nursing one of those big fruity rum drinks as he stares at everyone, especially Josh. A couple of women ask him to dance, and he brushes them off.

I see Josh, on the palace veranda, talking to Julissa. I can be quite stealthy when I want to be. I sneak up so I can hear what they're sayin'. "We're somethin', ain't we?" says Josh.

"That we are," says Julissa. "I want to help you, you want to help me. I'd do anything to help you get off this island...."

"Don't worry 'bout me," says Josh. "Worry 'bout yourself. You and your movie. So El Presidente still doesn't know..."

"No, but it's only a matter of time till one of his spies discovers what I'm up to. My only hope is to get the film out of the country, hopefully to America."

"How?"

"The same way *you're* getting out." Now they both laugh. Then they look at each other. Then they kiss. I back off. I hate mushy stuff. I see Cool Papa eating a big plate of spiced goat meat and mashed plantains, and I ask him if he knows what's going on.

"I know what you know," he says, shoveling the black, stringy mess into his mouth.

"We really gonna be here for the rest of our lives?" I ask.

"Maybe. Don't think so," he says

"Why not? Seems that way to me," I say. Cool Papa puts his fork down, smiles, and looks at me.

"Peanut," he says, "let me ask you a question."

"Okay."

"In the entire time we've been together, from that field down in Alabama where Josh almost got lynched to the time in the prison where we almost got shot to the last moment of the last game where we almost got shot again, has *anything* happened in the way you thought it would?" I think back.

"Actually, no," I answer.

"Then why would you expect this to be any different?" And with that, he walks back over to the buffet table to re-load his plate, and I just stand there staring into space. Man's got a point.

October 17, 1937

Four in the morning. The band's packed up, the buffet table is nothing but a five-foot stack of dirty dishes, and I'm with the fellas waiting out front of the palace for the bus back to the hotel. No more limousines. They were just for the newsreels when we first showed up. Now that the cameras are gone, the transportation has been downgraded to a single bus, but everybody's half asleep so it don't make no difference.

Dr. Enrique Aybar is there to shake everybody's hand as we all hop on the bus, with the biggest thank you for the last player to get on board. "Señor Gibson, our Exalted Benefactor has asked me to express his gratitude for the gracious way in which you accepted his invitation to represent the Dominican Republic on the diamond of baseball." Aybar shakes his hand, pauses, then shakes it again, and for the first time Aybar's little smile busts into a great big smile.

"Any place they throw money at me when I hit a homer, that feels like home," says Josh, smiling himself.

"Today shall be a day of rest. Tomorrow, we shall meet to plan El Presidente's world baseball tournament."

"Suits me," says Josh. They finally break off the handshake. Josh jumps on the bus, and I'm right behind him, followed by a single soldier from the Guardia Nacional. The door slams, and we're on our way.

Nobody says anything until Satch starts in on Josh. "You think Satchel's a fool, don't you, Josh?"

"Don't know what you mean," says Josh.

"You think ol' Satch is gonna work on Josh's Dominican baseball plantation, just 'cuz ol' Massa Josh done made a deal with El Presidente Grande Trujillo." Before Josh can answer, Cool Papa jumps in.

"Let's get something straight, Satch. When you jumped to the Sugar Kings, you just about got us all killed, including yourself. Whatever we do, we do as a team."

"Your lips to God's ear," says Deacon Powell, and everyone else pipes up in agreement.

"You boys want to waste your lives clownin' for these chili-pickers, that's up to you. Satchel's got better things to do. First chance he gets, Satchel's gonna say 'adios.' You boys be on your own."

The whole feeling in the bus changes in an instant. Nobody's drowsy now. All the fellas are sitting bolt upright, glowering at Satchel. What I was feeling turns out to be true – these guys weren't thrilled with the way Satch left them high and dry. Now that tiny spark of anger is a full flame of hostility.

"Satchel," says Cool Papa, "What you say is based on the idea that we just sit back and let you mess with us."

"I ain't messin' with you," says Satch.

"When you promise to win ball games for a guy who has got a shoot-first-and-ask-questions-later Secret Police force, and then you break that promise to work for the competition, yeah, that's messin' with us. That ain't gonna happen again," says Cool Papa.

"What are you gonna do? Shoot me?" smirks Satchel.

"Not that," says Josh. As usual, Satchel is blind to what's going on here. These fellas are mad. REAL mad, and he can't see it. I'm scared.

"What then?" asks Satch.

"Maybe we bust you up a little," says Cool Papa.

"Huh?"

"Not enough to kill you. Just break your arm, couple of fingers, just so's you can't use it to pitch for the other side, do us in a *second* time," says Josh. Satch looks at Josh, and then at Cool Papa. I can see what he's thinking. *"Holy cow, they really mean it."*

"Maybe ol' Satch was a little hasty," says Satch.

"Maybe ol' Satch needs to be taught a lesson," says Cool Papa.

"Satch don't need no lesson."

"We think he does," says Josh. "Don't we, fellas?" Every single player on the bus murmurs a yes. Now I see the Satch from the firing squad. He's actually scared.

"Look, fellas..." but before he can finish, they're on him – punching him, slapping him and beating on him. Josh is holding him from behind and the other guys are having at him. Holy cow! The Guardia Nacional soldier doesn't know what to do. He lets this go on for a couple of seconds, then he puts down his rifle and wades into this mess, trying to pry the guys off Satch.

The moment that soldier dives into the dogpile, Cool Papa jumps off and grabs his rifle. Bullet Hampton and Flash Fowler grab the soldier and get him in a death grip. He's so shocked he doesn't even struggle after his first reflexive lurch. Booker Samuels strips off his sidearm. Josh takes the pistol and moves to the bus driver. "Pull over," he says, putting the gun to the driver's head.

The only one more shocked than I am is Satch, who is backed up against his bus seat, arms up like he's still fending off blows. Satch and I both watch as the bus driver opens the door. I look out the window. We're somewhere in Ciudad Trujillo. The streets are stone dead, not a person in sight.

Josh moves to the soldier, whose eyes are wild with fright. "We ain't gonna hurt you, son," says Josh. "Get off the bus and go home. Don't do nothin' for a couple of hours, got it? We need a couple of hours. Then, if you got to, go to your Commandante and tell him what happened." The young soldier nods. "Out," says Josh. Bullet and Flash let him go, and the soldier starts toward the door of the bus. He stops when he gets to Cool Papa, who is holding the rifle.

"Sorry, son," he says, tightening his grip on the rifle, and the soldier trudges off the bus. Josh then guides the driver off the bus, nudging his head with the soldier's own pistol.

Josh springs back on the bus. Cool Papa Bell is in the driver's seat, just like back home. He starts to pull the door shut, but Josh puts his hand on Cool Papa's shoulder, then turns to Satch. "You want off, Satchel?"

"Huh?" says Satch, still dazed.

"You told us you were gonna say 'Adios' first chance you get," says Josh, moving over Satch. "Here's your chance. You want out, there's the door. No hard feelings." Satch's body doesn't move, just his head. He cocks that toward Josh.

"Didn't know you had a plan. Nobody told me," says Satch.

"We figured we were better off if you were in the dark," says Josh. "Yeah, we got a plan. The plan is to get off this damn island."

"Let's make for the dock," says Cool Papa. "That's where the Clipper is. That's our ticket outta here."

"That soldier boy's no fool," says Josh. "He ain't gonna wait to tell his boss. He's on his way right now to rat us out. When that happens, El Presidente Trujillo locks down that Clipper dock and we're stuck here."

"Okay," says Booker. "So how does having this bus help us one little bit?" Josh smiles, and pulls a map out of his back pocket. He pulls out the accordion folds until the map is totally open, so everyone can see.

"Here's where we are -- Ciudad Trujillo, right about here." Now he slides his finger to the right. "Cool Papa, you need to get us here -- Marena Beach, in San Pedro de Macoris."

"And what's there that ain't here?" asks Cool Papa.

"A nice big boat, property of our new best friend, Mister Tyler Underwood," says Josh, with a great big smile. "I made a deal with him at the party. When we get back to the States, he's got us for one year. We're the Josh Gibson All-Stars, sponsored by American Sugar. He pays all our expenses, and takes 90% of what we make." All eyes swivel to Satchel, including Josh's. "You down with that, Satch?"

"I got a choice?" he says.

"There's the door. You can get off now."

"No thanks."

"So you're in?" says Josh.

"I'm in," says Satch. And with that, Cool Papa yanks the door shut and flattens the accelerator. That bus lurches forward, throwing us back against our seats. Bumpin' down a pot-holed road in the pitch-black night – feels like I'm back home already.

We get to Marena Beach just as the first streaks of orange light are telling everyone -- including the Guardia Nacional -- that a new day has arrived. Our transport to Catalina Island, where the Clipper is docked, is Underwood's personal runabout, a dinky nineteen foot Chris Craft motorboat with two rows of seats that each fit three guys, including the Skipper. We've got ten guys. Three cram in next to the Skipper up front, four stuff themselves in the seat just behind them, and three more -- Willie Tatum, Cool Papa Bell, and yours truly -- lay out flat on the back deck, our fingers hooked onto the decorative brass rail above the rear seat. "HOLD ON!" screams the Skipper as he turns the "Sugar King" around. The poor boat is so over-loaded that it barely bobs above the water line, and water sloshes over me as we putter off towards who knows where. My mouth fills with salty water as my knuckles turn white from holding onto that rail. I have one picture in my mind -- those shark noses bobbing up and down ready to rip into their next meal.

CHAPTER TWENTY-EIGHT

"There it is!" shouts Cool Papa. "Hold on, Peanut!" I look up and see it – the Pan Am Clipper, dead ahead! This is the very first time I let myself believe that we have even the tiniest chance of getting back to Pittsburgh in one piece.

About ten minutes later our little boat finally docks under the wing of the Clipper. I slide off into some shallow water and dog paddle up onto shore along with the rest of the fellas, who are chest deep in the water, wrecking what's left of their fine tuxedos. Tyler Underwood is there on the dock smoking a Lucky Strike. He strides up and shakes Josh's hand. "Welcome to Catalina Island. You boys look like you've had a long night."

"Mister Underwood, the fellas are pretty anxious to put this place in our rear view mirror," says Josh. "So if you've got that contract..."

Underwood pulls the contract out of the back pocket of his white trousers and hands it to Josh. "Here you go, Josh." He hands Josh a pen just as

Satchel tries to grab the contract, but Cool Papa gets his hands on it first. He hands it to Booker, who scans it with Josh, Satch, and Cool Papa crowding over his shoulder. All three come to the offending paragraph at the same moment.

"Whoa, whoa, whoa!" says Booker.

"Hold on!" says Satch.

"What?" says Tyler, innocent as a newborn babe.

"I think your secretary made a small typographical error, Mister Underwood," says Booker.

"Error? I don't..."

"Right here, where it says how long we're obligated to play for American Sugar," says Booker.

"Where there should be a '1.' Somehow, a zero has mysteriously appeared. Says '10,'" says Josh

"Does it really?" says Underwood. He's trying hard to act surprised, and fooling nobody.

"It does really," says Cool Papa.

"So if you'll just hand me that fine fountain pen, we'll just cross off that zero, and then we'll be all set," says Josh. Underwood smiles. Not a mean smile. More of a "let's really get down to business" smile.

"Well, here's the way I figure it, boys." He lights a fresh cigarette with the smoldering butt of the last one and inhales deeply. "I figure I'm your best and only hope of getting out of here in one piece. Because if you don't sign that contract, I get on that plane by myself. And then Trujillo will find you and kill you, or throw you in prison for those same ten years, letting you out to play baseball for him. I figure ten years playing for American Sugar back in the states is a small price to pay for your lives."

"Ten years," says Satch, "is mostly likely the best part of Satchel's career, if he's lucky. Same goes for Josh and Cool Papa. That means American Sugar has us for the rest of our baseball lives."

"Yeah," says Underwood, "That's a good deal for us."

"Yeah. In the same way that slavery was a good deal for plantation owners," says Booker. Underwood knits his brow.

"Slaves didn't have any choice. No contract. You boys don't want to sign, don't sign. But you'll sign all right."

"Why's that?" says Josh, glowering.

"Because, Josh, you've got no choice." Underwood smiles. Josh steps forward, till he's almost nose-to-nose with Underwood. The smile vanishes. Josh turns to me.

"Peanut, what do you think?"

I think back over everything that's happened to us. "What I think…is that we always got a choice. We don't have to give in to evil. We can fight it."

"Good," says Josh as he takes the contract out of Booker's hands. "Mr. Underwood, we made a deal." Josh folds the contract, opens Underwood's coat and sticks it into his inside pocket. "You bring me that deal, we'll sign it."

"Sorry," says Underwood, staring at Josh, "That was then, this is now. Good luck to you. You'll need it." He turns to Satch. "Satch? What say you and me get on that plane. We'll figure out our own deal on the way back to Miami." Satch looks at Underwood, and then at Josh.

"I'm, uh....I'm part of the team, Mister Underwood. What Josh says goes." What a change! Josh smiles. Underwood looks at him for a long moment, like he thinks this might one of Satchel's jokes. Then he sees the situation for what it is. Things have changed.

"Suit yourself," says Underwood. And he turns toward the door of the Clipper just as the first rifle round zings that fine Panama hat right off his head.

Every head swivels toward the source of the shot. A Dominican Coast Guard boat is bouncing toward us. Three sharpshooters are out front, trying to get a bead on us. Right behind them, yelling and pointing, is the Maximum Leader himself, Dr. Rafael Trujillo. Suddenly I'm being yanked toward the Clipper. Josh has my arm and he's running full tilt, just ahead of the rest of the fellas, right behind Cool Papa, with a panicked Underwood bringing up the rear. We clamber up the stairway as rifle bullets pee-wang off the aluminum skin of the Clipper. Door slams shut and engines rev full tilt. Everybody jockeys for a peek out a window as the Clipper wallows into the ocean.

The Coast Guard boat roars right up to our plane, with Trujillo screaming at his riflemen to stop us.

Only problem is the awesome prop-wash of those four massive radial engines. Trujillo's boat bobs up and down like a toy in a bathtub, and the riflemen fall back just as Trujillo himself steps up. He's holding a Thompson submachine gun, like the kind Jimmy Cagney uses in gangster movies. "EVERYBODY DOWN!" yells Josh as he crashes to the floor directly on top of me. Before I can yelp I hear PING-PING-PING-PING-PING-PING-PING as machine gun bullets rip through the fuselage just above the windows. I can feel the kick and hear the smash of waves on the bottom of the plane as we pick up speed, and then -- we're airborne. Nobody gets off the floor for at least a minute. Finally, Cool Papa gets up and looks out his window.

"Coast is clear. He's out of ammo. He's just shaking his fist at us." Only then does Josh get up off me.

"You okay, Peanut?" asks Josh.

"Yeah, I guess." I take the window seat, and he sits next to me.

Underwood makes one half-hearted attempt to talk to Josh about signing that one-year contract to play for American Sugar, but Josh just tells him he'll have to think about it, which is a lot more polite than yelling, "What?!? After that jive you pulled back there?" Underwood says, "No hard feelings. Just business," and sits down next to Cool Papa.

"So," Josh finally says to me as we tuck into our tenderloin steaks, "What are you gonna tell your mama about our little vacation?"

"Well," I say between bites of fried potato, "I'm not sure. What do you think I should I tell her?"

"Tell her we had ourselves a fine time playing for the best fans in the world. And that Josh Gibson said you were the best batboy in Crawfords history."

"In other words," I say, "Leave out the sharks."

"She wouldn't believe it anyway." He turns back to his steak, but I keep looking at him.

"Thanks, Josh. I ain't the same as I was when I left. I got a whole different way of lookin' at things. I owe that to you."

"I told your mama I'd look after you."

"And you did. Big time."

EPILOGUE

I'd seen a lot in the Dominican Republic -- the best and worst humanity had to offer. I'd taken a gander at what pure evil looks like, and I'd seen what a good man can do when he stares fear in the face, reaches into himself, and does the right thing for the right reason.

After what I'd gone through, I couldn't go back to my life as a scared little numbers runner for Gus Greenlee. Now I wanted more than money. I knew I had to do something with my life, make a real difference. If it involved knocking down the walls of race prejudice that kept Josh Gibson in baseball jail, that would be just fine with me.

Cool Papa Bell introduced me to a sports reporter named Wendell Smith, who worked for the *Pittsburgh Courier*, a paper read by every black person in the country. I quit Greenlee and took a job as a copy boy, working after school. (Yes, I went back to school.) I made such a pest of myself that the *Courier* promoted me – made me a full-fledged (cub) reporter on my 21st birthday, just to get me out of the office. I helped push the paper's "Double V" campaign, which took the "V for Victory" drive in World War II and added another V -- victory over race prejudice. The paper demanded that black soldiers who risked their lives on the front lines in Europe and Japan be given full citizenship rights at home. (Yes, this was actually controversial at the time. Times change, thank God.)

I worked with Wendell on a campaign to integrate major league baseball. On April 15, 1947 Wendell and I were two of 26,623 fans screaming our heads off at Ebbets Field as a Brooklyn first sacker named Jackie Roosevelt Robinson finally smashed through the color line. That day was both thrilling and sad, because the man who saved my life, the great Josh Gibson, had passed away three months earlier on January 20th, at the age of 35. After the game Wendell and I shared beers on the train back to Pittsburgh. "Should have been Josh," said Wendell.

"The black Babe Ruth," I said. "Never would have happened without him." Every time Jackie came to bat, I saw Josh in a Brooklyn Dodgers uniform, rolling up his right sleeve and standing stock still at the plate, daring the pitcher to throw him a strike. Jackie was under a lot of pressure, but Josh? He played for his life.

I always viewed my job at the newspaper as "storyteller." I told Jackie Robinson's story as he changed America by changing baseball. I told Martin

Luther King's story as he changed the meaning of "We, the People" to mean ALL the people. And now I've finally been able to tell Josh Gibson's story.

He changed my life by showing me what real courage looks like.

AUTHOR FACT AND FICTION QUESTIONS AND ANSWERS

"What actually happened? What did I invent?"

Q: Some of the events in the book seem a little incredible – firing squads? Evil dictators ordering mass murder? Victims fed to the sharks? And yet you claim this is "based on a true story." So what in *Sugarball* is fact and what is fiction?

A: Researching this book was my hobby for more than ten years, and I enjoyed every minute. (Sometimes I think I write books just so I have an excuse to read other books and find things out.)

Like most great historical "yarns," some of the most outlandish stuff in *Sugarball* is true. Truth, as they say, is definitely stranger than fiction. Let's go through the book and you'll see what I mean.

CHAPTER ONE

Q: Were the Pittsburgh Crawfords a real Negro League team, and were they owned by a numbers "kingpin" named Gus Greenlee?

A: True. Many Negro League teams were owned by underworld figures like Gus Greenlee. In the Jim Crow 1930s, many legitimate business opportunities were closed to African-Americans. Greenlee "moved in the shadows" because that's where the money was. He made his first big score during Prohibition as a bootlegger, and then moved into the numbers business after Prohibition was repealed.

The Pittsburgh Crawfords were not only a real team; they were the *premiere* team in the Negro Leagues in the mid 1930s. Many baseball historians rank the 1935-37 Crawfords in the top 10 professional baseball teams of all time. Some rank them as the best team ever.

At most times in Negro League history, one team dominated the league. In the mid-1930s, it was the Crawfords. From the late 1930s through the 1940s, it was the Kansas City Monarchs. There are two reasons for this.

First, the real money for Negro League teams was in "barnstorming" – touring the country playing non-league exhibition games in front of hometown crowds. A team like the Crawfords might play more than 200 games a year, but only 40 or 50 as part of the official Negro National League. Only a de facto

"All-Star" team with marketable stars like Satchel Paige and Josh Gibson could become a national gate attraction.

Second, Negro League owners knew that at some point the baseball establishment would bow to the inevitable and integrate the major leagues. The Negro League owners miscalculated the method, however. They thought that white owners would integrate by incorporating one all-Negro team into the league. The Negro League owners had an informal agreement that if the Crawfords (or, later, the Monarchs) were accepted into the major leagues, all the owners would benefit financially. They were shocked when Branch Rickey integrated the Dodgers with Jackie Robinson. And they were mortified when Rickey and the other white owners then raided the Negro Leagues for the best players, and refused to recognize existing Negro League contracts.

CHAPTER FOUR

Q: Did Negro League players actually barnstorm against teams of white teams, like the Dizzy Dean All-Stars?

A: Just as I was completing my manuscript, Timothy M. Gay came out with an excellent book called *Satch, Dizzy and Rapid Robert – The Wild Saga of Interracial Baseball Before Jackie Robinson.* Yes, much to the consternation of Baseball Commissioner (and intractable racist) Kennesaw Mountain Landis, teams of white "All-Stars" played exhibition games against the best players in the Negro Leagues. I tried to depict one of these games accurately.

Q: Satchel Paige's outrageous routine of bringing in the outfielders, telling the batter what he was going to throw and reducing the size of home plate to a sliver of chewing gum wrapper on the plate – true?

A: True. Satchel Paige was more than the greatest baseball pitcher of his time. He was also an accomplished showman -- the only Negro League player whose name alone could guarantee a healthy gate for an exhibition game. In his must-read biography of Paige, *Satchel – The Life and Times of an American Legend* Larry Tye reports that Paige's presence on the field was good for an additional two thousand fans when black All-Stars took on white teams.

CHAPTER SIX

Q: Did Negro League teams actually have to camp out when they barnstormed through the South? And when they did, did they ever camp together with Negro big bands, like that of Cab Calloway?

A: One of my research sources was *Invisible Men -- Life in Baseball's Negro Leagues* by Donn Rogosin. This, from page 131, in the chapter "On the Road":

"The Kansas City Monarchs' solution to prejudice in lodging was to camp out. The sight of several old Dodge cars loaded with tents, cots, blankets, cooking utensils, and a team of wandering black ballplayers was a sight indeed."

Black big bands like Cab Calloway's had the same problem as Negro League baseball teams. Black bands had to tour to make a living, as these bands couldn't get booked into the more prestigious (white, segregated) hotels and on lucrative national radio shows that helped finance white bands like those of Tommy Dorsey, Artie Shaw, and Glenn Miller. A black big band might do 300 one-nighters a year, and that would take them into areas in the South where camping might be the only option. To avoid attacks from racist groups like the Ku Klux Klan, black bands and black baseball teams would find safety in numbers by camping together.

Final note – eight black men were lynched in the United States in 1937. (http://www.law.umkc.edu/faculty/projects/ftrials/shipp/lynchingyear.html) This is down from the appalling high of 161 black lynchings in 1892, but still shocking and tragic.

CHAPTER SEVEN

Q: Were white major league teams really interested in giving black players try-outs as early as 1937?

A: First, a caveat -- in my book, the Washington Senators never intend to give Paige, Gibson, and Bell a real tryout. The owner just wants them to anchor his "Zulu Cannibal Team." (see next question).

That said, the real story of baseball integration begins in the 1930s with Lester Rodney. In the book, *Press Box Red – The Story of Lester Rodney, the Communist Who Helped Break the Color Line in American Sports,* I learned how Rodney, as sports reporter for the Communist newspaper *The Daily Worker,* began agitating for the integration of baseball. (The character in the book named Toby Dakota is based on Lester Rodney.) Soon black newspapers joined *The Daily Worker* in trying to get major league teams to offer tryouts to black players.

By the early 1940s, some owners were showing a little interest. Here's a quote from *When the Game Was Black and White* by Bruce Chadwick:

"Clark Griffith, owner of the Washington Senators, was a regular fan at black ball games staged in his ballpark (which brought him thousands in rental fees) and was impressed by the Negro Leaguers. In 1942 he called Bell and Gibson up to his office, talked for a half hour with them, and went so far as to ask them if they were interested in playing for the Senators, prompting rumors that he would sign them. He did not. Earlier, in 1938, he had reputedly told friends that he was going to sign Satchel Paige for $75,000 a year. Prominent Washingtonians talked him out of it, reminding him that Washington was very much a 'southern town.'"

Q: You have Calvin Griffith asking Paige, Gibson, and Bell if they'd be interested in fronting a "Zulu Cannibal" barnstorming team. Were there really such teams?

A: You betcha. From page 94 in *When the Game Was Black and White*:

"And, of course, then there were the Zulu Cannibal Giants Baseball Tribe, which barnstormed around the country, playing in African tribal paints and hula skirts. The brainchild of New York promoter Syd Pollock, the Zulu Giants were scorned by the serious black ballplayers because they conjured

up all of the stereotypes about blacks these same players were trying to erase with their bats and gloves. But Pollock and the team attracted plenty of attention."

CHAPTER EIGHT

Q: What about Dr. Enrique Aybar? Was this a real person? Did he actually come to America and offer Satchel all that cash money?

A: True – however, there is some controversy about how the money was delivered. Here's what Larry Tye says in *Satchel*:

"Everywhere Satchel went in New Orleans he ran into agents whose Panama hats and cream-colored suits betrayed them as Latin even if he mistook them for Haitian. Finally Aybar cornered him, blocking Satchel's car with his black limousine and by one account pulling a pistol to focus the pitcher's attention. 'We will give you thirty thousand American dollars for you and eight teammates,' Satchel remembered Aybar telling him, 'and you may take what you feel is your share.' That was more money for a month's work than even Satchel made for a year of backbreaking barnstorming, and in today's dollars would be $440,000."

Here's how Satch remembered the incident in his autobiography, *Maybe I'll Pitch Forever*:

"'Thirty thousand?' I asked.

'Yes. Thirty thousand.' (said Dr. Aybar)

"Do I get to see the money?" I asked then. I'd been roped in on too many of those big deals and then ended up without a penny and this kind of smelled like one of them. I wasn't going to jump a good job like I had with the Crawfords, not without some hard money in my pocket.

'I'll be back tomorrow,' he told me.

The next day he was back and handed me a bankbook. He'd put thirty thousand in that bank for me."

So where did the suitcase come from? Here's yet another version of the story, from *Josh and Satch – The Life and Times of Josh Gibson and Satchel Paige* by John B. Holway:

"The Trujillo team, the Dragones, pursued him to spring training in New Orleans, cornered him on the street with a big, black limousine, pulled a pistol, according to one account, opened up a suitcase with $30,000 in bills, and told him to pick eight other players at $3,000 each and keep the change."

One final version of the story, from Rogosin's *Invisible Men*:

"Catching up with Paige in New Orleans, Trujillo's men offered a large sum of money to Paige,

a man with a notorious love of cold cash. The rather crude but effective Dominican technique involved spreading large amounts of greenbacks on a bed and encouraging the recruit to take his specified amount as an advance."

So what's true? Bank book? Suitcase? Greenbacks on a bed? I can't find a definitive first-person account, but I'm certain that Aybar came to the United States, found Paige, and put cash in his hands to get him to jump the Crawfords and travel to the Dominican Republic.

Q: Was it a two team, five-game baseball tournament?

A: No. Here I took some license. In fact, the tournament lasted from March 28 to July 11. It involved three teams – the Dragones from Ciudad Trujillo, the Estrellas Orientales of San Pedro de Macoris, and the Aguilas Cibaeñas of Santiago.

At some point, the Estrellas Orientales were eliminated, and Ciudad Trujillo and Santiago played an eight-game series for the championship. The Paige/Gibson/Bell team won the first four games. Santiago came back to win the next two. Ciudad Trujillo won the fifth game 8-6, with Paige on the mound in the ninth inning.

Q: Which players actually went to the Dominican Republic?

A: Here again I changed things for dramatic purposes. Satchel Paige, Josh Gibson, and Cool Papa Bell all made the trip. The others were Herman Andrew, Sam Bankhead, Bob Griffith, Leroy Matlock, Cy Perkins, and Harry Williams.

My characters -- Payday Thompson, "Deacon" Powell, Willie Tatum, "Bullet" Hampton, "Flash" Fowler, and Booker Samuels -- are characters I made up. Several of these characters are based on real Negro League players. For example, "Deacon" Powell's religious leanings were borrowed from William Greason, a Negro League player in the late 40s and early 50s who later became Pastor of the Bethel Baptist Church in Birmingham, Alabama.

Q: When the players arrive in Ciudad Trujillo, they are bombarded by pro-Trujillo propaganda. Everywhere they turn, they see Trujillo glorifying himself. Is this an accurate account of the way things were in the Dominican Republic in 1937?

A: Yes. Rafael Trujillo was absolute dictator of the Dominican Republic, and, like most dictators, orchestrated his own public adoration. Everything Peanut sees on the way from the airplane to the first rally is accurate – the many statues, the parks, streets and plazas named for Trujillo, the billboards calling him "Exalted Benefactor of the People" and the church banners reading "God in Heaven, Trujillo on Earth." (Churches were, of course, required to fly these banners.)

CHAPTER ELEVEN

Q: When the players arrive, Satchel is horrified to learn that Trujillo is "asking" (i.e., demanding) that the players kick back 10% of their salaries. Is this how Trujillo operated?

A: True. On August 16, 1931, one year after his inauguration, Trujillo outlawed all political parties except his, the Dominican Party. All party members and all government employees "donated" 10 percent of their salary to Trujillo's regime. An important reason to join the party was the "palmita" – the party membership card that protected you from being arrested on trumped-up charges.

CHAPTER TWELVE

Q: Was Maximo Borgatti a real character?

A: Borgatti is fictional, but the terrifying organizations that Borgatti heads were real. Borgatti is the Chief of the Guardia Nacional, the massive military organization dedicated to keeping Trujillo in power. He is also head of the Military Intelligence

Service, a secret police force similar to the Gestapo in Germany. This Service spied on people, controlled the press, extorted money from businesses, and jailed (and sometimes murdered) those suspected of opposing Trujillo.

Trujillo studied and emulated his better-known counterparts as they came to power – Francisco Franco in Spain, Mussolini in Italy, and Hitler in Germany. He used the same strategies and methods of intimidation and terror that they did.

CHAPTER THIRTEEN

Q: Was Julissa Perez a real person?

A: She is fictional. In my book, she is making a documentary film about Trujillo in order to burnish his legend around the world. Trujillo studied the methods that Adolf Hitler used to gain and keep power. Hitler's Nazi Party hired a talented filmmaker named Leni Riefenstahl to make a documentary glorifying Hitler. The film, *Triumph of the Will* is one of the greatest (and most notorious) propaganda films of all time. I figured Trujillo might order a similar work of cinematic self-glorification.

CHAPTER FOURTEEN

Q: Did Trujillo's team have to face a team made up of Cuban "ringers?"

A: Here again I took a bit of license (but only a bit). All three teams in the real tournament vied for the best players from around the world. Each team had players from the Dominican Republic, the Negro Leagues, and Cuba. For the record, Martin Dihigo was a real player – a legend who could both pitch and hit. In fact, in the Dominican series, Dihigo finished second to Satchel Paige in pitching victories, and second to Josh Gibson in batting average!

CHAPTER FIFTEEN

Q: Were the Crawfords actually threatened by a firing squad?

A: Here's what Donn Rogosin said in *Invisible Men*:

"Another time, when Trujillo's team lost a series to Santiago, his players returned to their hotel to discover a squad of angry militiamen. 'El Presidente doesn't lose,' shouted the militiamen, firing their rifles in the air. 'You know you are playing for el Presidente,' they shouted, and more shots rang out. Cool Papa Bell and other Ciudad Trujillo Negro leaguers were terrified, and they swept their next series against Santiago."

I found some version of this in virtually every account of the Crawfords' adventures in the Dominican Republic. I'm convinced the players thought their lives were in danger. Here's Cool Papa Bell, from a 1973 article called "No Place In The Shade" by Mark Kram in *Sports Illustrated*:

"We found out that, as far as Trujillo was concerned, we either won or we were going to lose big. That means he was going to kill us."

CHAPTER NINETEEN

Q: Was Tyler Underwood a real person? Did the American sugar interests finance one of the other teams?

A: Here again, I mixed fact and fiction. By 1937, Trujillo had nationalized virtually every business in the Dominican Republic *except* sugar. Trujillo and his family had monopoly control of the meat industry (i.e., slaughterhouses), milk, tobacco, cement, chocolate, alcohol, paint, and textiles. Trujillo was far and away the largest landowner in the Dominican. He had been put in power by the American military acting on behalf of American sugar interests.

As much as he wanted those money-spinning sugar plantations, Trujillo had to be careful. My fictional American sugar baron, Mr. Underwood, would certainly have been uneasy about Trujillo. Trujillo's government was a "kleptocracy," dedicated to looting the country as quickly and thoroughly as possible. How long until Trujillo went after "big sugar?" Tyler Underwood was trying to head off the inevitable, and replace Trujillo with someone more compliant to his own corporate interests.

CHAPTER TWENTY

Q: Did Satchel Paige really "jump" the Dominican national team and pitch for a rival?

A: This is the biggest fictional leap I took in the book. No, he didn't. He played with the "Dragones" the whole tournament.

I justified this move two ways. First, the rivalry between Satch and Josh was real. They were great friends, but each thought he was the best at what he did. Each thought he could win a head-to-head battle with the other. I wanted to see that battle play itself out.

Second, Satchel's jump to the Sugar Kings for a big paycheck was true to his character. Here's how Cool Papa Bell put it in Rogosin's *Invisible Men*:

"Now Satchel was the type of guy that if you showed him money – or a car – you could lead him anywhere. He was that type of fella. He did a lot of wrong things in baseball, but he was easily led."

I'm not trying to judge Satchel here. He was an entrepreneur in a very tough business, in a very tough time for African-Americans. He wanted to control his own fate. He'd happily sign a contract with someone like Gus Greenlee, and then just as happily jump (as he did in 1935) to a team in North Dakota for more money. It should be noted that Satchel had good reason to look out for himself. Negro League owners were notorious for tearing up contracts and abandoning players who were injured – refusing to honor their commitments, just putting them off the bus wherever they were on the road.

CHAPTER TWENTY TWO

Q: Did Trujillo really order the killing of 17,000 Haitians? Were the bodies really fed to sharks?

A: Yes. This terrible crime is called "The Parsley Massacre" because of the way the victims were identified. It began on October 3, 1937. Guardia Nacional soldiers poured into the border area dividing the Dominican Republic and Haiti. They confronted dark-skinned Haitian migrant workers, held up sprigs of parsley and asked, "What is this called?" If the answer came back "Pe'sil" instead of "Perejil," the victim would be murdered with a machete. (Haitians couldn't sound the trilled "r" of "perejil.") The Haitians were hacked to death instead of shot so that Trujillo could tell the world the victims were killed by Dominican cane workers, defending themselves. Once they were murdered, the bodies of the workers were taken to the Atlantic Ocean and thrown to the sharks.

Trujillo was a racist. He admired the insane racial theories of Adolf Hitler. In a move that echoes today's anti-immigration border politics, Trujillo was trying to distract his people from their Depression economic woes. He wanted to stir up resentment against the Haitians by blaming them for taking the jobs of Dominican cane workers. He also claimed that the Haitians threatened the superior racial bloodlines of the Dominican people.

An excellent fictional account of this holocaust is *The Farming of Bones* by the Haitian-American writer Edwidge Danticat.

Final note – The Negro League players were never involved in any of the "Parsley Massacre" events, although both the baseball tournament and the massacre took place in 1937.

CHAPTER TWENTY THREE

Q: The final game -- Were the players really playing for their lives? Were there Dominican soldiers on the field?

A: I would give this question a qualified "yes." Here's how Satchel described the scene in *Maybe I'll Pitch Forever*:

"Some of them guys the president had watching us would have made those bums back in the states look like schoolteachers. They were that tough looking. They all had guns and long knives stuck in their belts.

When we got to the park for the championship game, our manager got us all together before we went out on the field. 'You better win,' he said.

'What'a you mean, we better win?' I asked.

'I mean just that. Take my advice and win.'

But by the seventh inning we were a run behind and you could see Trujillo lining up his army. They began to look like a firing squad.

In the last of the seventh we scored two runs and went ahead, six to five. You never saw Ol' Satch throw harder after that. I shut them out the last two innings and we'd won.

I hustled back to the hotel and the next morning we blowed out of there in a hurry.

We never did see Trujillo again. I ain't sorry."

Virtually every account of the game includes the warning from the manager, the soldiers on the field, and the presence of Trujillo, who was in a fight for his political life and had no qualms about ordering those who betrayed him to be murdered.

CHAPTER TWENTY FOUR

Q: What happened after the last game?

A: In his autobiography, Satchel says, "I hustled back to our hotel and we blowed out of there in a hurry. We never did see Trujillo again. I ain't sorry." Larry Tye's biography of Satchel presents this version, and then presents alternate versions from Satchel himself. One version has him staying three days, and another has him lingering in the Dominican Republic for as long as two months.

Q: What happened to Satchel Paige? Josh Gibson? Cool Papa Bell?

A: Sadly, the Dominican series marked the last time that Satchel Paige and Josh Gibson played as teammates. Satchel Paige finally broke into the major leagues on July 9, 1948 with the Cleveland Indians. He was, at age 42, the oldest rookie in big league history. He went 6-1, with a sterling 2.48 earned run average, and then helped the Indians win the World Series in six games.

Paige continued to pitch professionally until 1966. He was elected to the Baseball Hall of Fame in 1971. There's lots of great stuff out there about Satchel. Start with Larry Tye's biography, and go from there.

James Thomas "Cool Papa" Bell had a long, productive career as a player that lasted until 1946. He's one of those amazing Negro League legends whose incredible exploits seem too good to be true. *Did he really (as Ken Burns said in his famous* Baseball *documentary series) score from first base on a sacrifice bunt? Could he really circle the bases in eleven seconds? Was he really called out because he was hit by his own batted ball as he slid into second?*

After he stopped playing, he coached for the Kansas City Monarchs, and managed their "B" team. After baseball was integrated, Bell became a scout and teacher, tutoring future greats like Jackie Robinson, Elston Howard, and Ernie Banks. He was elected to the Hall of Fame in 1974, and passed away in Kansas City in 1991, at the age of 87.

Josh Gibson had a much sadder life. How good was he? Here's the great Bill James, from his *New Historical Baseball Abstract*, my favorite book of baseball history:

"Probably the greatest catcher in baseball history, and probably the greatest right-handed power hitter. Bill Veeck said that Gibson was the greatest hitter he ever saw. So did countless other Negro League participants and observers."

Gibson was diagnosed with a malignant brain tumor in 1943, but continued to play baseball. He died of a stroke in 1947, at age 35, three months before Jackie Robinson broke baseball's color line. He was elected to the Hall of Fame in 1972, a year after Satchel Paige.

I invite every reader of this book to find out more about these great players, and other Negro League legends. I include a bibliography of my research. I'm certain you'll be amazed by the true-life exploits of these men.

A lot of fans today complain about spoiled, overpaid sports stars. The Negro Leaguers played under grim, often horrific conditions for almost no money and very little fame. They truly played for the love of the game.

BIBLIOGRAPHY

Bruce, Janet. *The Kansas City Monarchs – Champions of Black Baseball*, Lawrence, Kansas, The University Press of Kansas, 1985

Chadwick, Bruce. *When the Game Was Black and White*, New York, Abbeville Press, 1992

Dixon, Phil (with Patrick J. Hannigan). *The Negro Baseball Leagues – A Photographic History*, Mattituck, New York, Amereon House, 1992

Gay, Timothy. *Satch, Dizzy and Rapid Robert – The Wild Saga of Interracial Baseball Before Jackie Robinson*, New York, Simon & Schuster, 2010

Hogan, Lawrence D. *Shades of Glory – The Negro Leagues and the Story of African-American Baseball*, Washington D.C., National Geographic, 2006

Holway, John B. *Blackball Stars – Negro League Pioneers*, New York, Carroll & Graf, 1992

Holway, John B. *Josh and Satch – The Life and Times of Josh Gibson and Satchel Paige*, New York, Carroll & Graf, 1991

Holway, John B. *Voices from the Great Black Baseball Leagues*, Revised Edition, New York, De Capo Press, 1992

James, Bill. *The New Bill James Historical Baseball Abstract*, New York, The Free Press, 2001

Peterson, Robert. *Only The Ball Was White*, New York, Oxford University Press, 1992

Paige, Leroy (Satchel) (as told to David Lipman). *Maybe I'll Pitch Forever*, New York: Doubleday, 1962

Ribowsky, Mark. *The Power And The Darkness – The Life of Josh Gibson In The Shadows Of The Game*, New York, Simon and Schuster, 1996

Riley, James A. *The Biographical Encyclopedia of The Negro Baseball Leagues,* New York: Carroll & Graf, 1994

Rogosin, Donn. *Invisible Men – Life in Baseball's Negro Leagues*, New York, Atheneum, 1983

Silber, Irwin. *Press Box Red – The Story of Lester Rodney, The Communist Who Helped Break The*

Color Line In American Sports, Philadelphia, Temple University Press, 2003

Tye, Larry. *Satchel – The Life and Times of an American Legend*, New York, Random House, 2009

ABOUT THE AUTHOR

R. Lee Procter is a writer and amateur baseball scholar living in the Los Angeles area. He has won a number of awards for his advertising work. He has written and produced hundreds of hours of television. He currently works as a writer in the themed entertainment business, creating museum exhibits, stadium tours and guest narratives for brand homes. He stumbled across this story when it was mentioned in the Ken Burns *Baseball* documentary. A single ten second mention led him on a remarkable two year adventure. He's happy that the heroism of these legendary players can be properly acknowledged and celebrated.

NOTE FROM THE AUTHOR

Word-of-mouth is crucial for any author to succeed. If you enjoyed *Sugarball*, please leave a review online—anywhere you are able. Even if it's just a sentence or two. It would make all the difference and would be very much appreciated.

Thanks!
R. Lee Procter